Preface

Poetry has always been my first love and Urdu poetry has fascinated me the most. Urdu poetry casts a spell which poetry in no other language does. I remember when as a schoolboy I first read :

उम्रे-दराज़ मांगकर लाये थे चार दिन
दो आरज़ू में कट गये दो इन्तज़ार में

I was in a state of daze for good eight days. The sheer wit of it and the tragic tinge therein so well fused, I don't find it, say in English poetry (excepting Shakespeare) which I have read and taught all my life and which I have been writing for some time now. If this is one's experience with Bahadur Shah Zafar, who is not among the greatest of the Urdu poets, it is not difficult to imagine how would one respond to Ghalib, Meer, Faiz or Iqbal. I have virtually lived with them, enjoying them immensely, moved, comforted and uplifted by them. If Ghalib has a couplet for every situation in our daily lives, Iqbal can infuse life even in a dying man, and if Meer can teach you how to illuminate an abstract idea by illustrating it with images and allusions from ordinary life, Faiz moves you with his lyrical sweetness, rousing you at the same time to fight injustice and oppression. Apart from these great names, some of the later poets like Parvin Shakir and Ahmed Faraz (both from Pakistan) are remarkable for their freshness, depth and awareness. And then there is a long list of good poets.

However, much as I have loved Urdu poetry, I had never thought of translating it into English The encouragement for it came from my publisher Shri Vishwa Nath ji who is a connoisseur of poetry and a good poet himself. Also I had all along felt the need for an anthology of Urdu poetry in English translation for the benefit of readers who are not so well versed in Urdu. Preparing such an anthology I knew, was an uphill task, particularly because where poetry is concerned, I am bit of a perfectionist. And I cannot reconcile to the idea of a translation of ghazals and nazms which merely conveys the meaning of the original and is as such not much better than a prose rendering of them. Translation of poetry from one language to the other is extremely difficult, some would say, impossible. The challenge here is the challenge of being faithful to the original and at the same time retaining at least some of its charm and beauty. It is not only the idea of the original that is to be conveyed but its soul, its strength, its poignancy and sweetness, and if possible, its rhythm and resonance should also reach the reader. As Sheffered Peach said, "Translation is not just translating ideas from one language to the other, a good translation is akin to the original, even better". The challenge is that in the translation also, it must read like good poetry. And the challenge is particularly tough in the case of the ghazal. One of the ways I could think of meeting this challenge is to translate the verses in rhymed couplets provided the rhymes are not laboured.

I started on the project with Ghalib and got so immersed in the poetry of the great man that the number of pieces translated went on increasing till it became a separate book 'Diwan-e-Ghalib, A Selection.' For the present anthology, I have selected thirty four poets from Meer Taqi Meer to Ahmed Faraz and Shaharyar. Needless to say, some important names have remained unrepresented. This is because the number of good poets is so large that it is very difficult to include them all. Also, I have had to make a rigorous selection of verses even within a single ghazal so that only the best reaches the readers.

Besides Vishwa Nath ji, I thank Dr. Khalid Ashraf of the Urdu Department, Kirori mal College, Delhi University for his invaluable help in preparing the anthology. He has read through and corrected the manuscript and made valuable suggestions.

Thanks are also due to Mr. Khushwant Singh for his encouraging words. When I sent to him three or four of my pieces for opinion, he wrote *"You have done a superb job of 'Abhi to main Jawan hoon'. I tried my hand at it and published the first half in my column. It was not half as good as yours. Majaz and Sahir are also well done"*. I thank Mr. Mithuraaj Dhusiya, Shri O.P. Sapra and Shri Rahul Gupta for their help in preparing the manuscript. Also to be thanked are my daughters, Ritu Dewan and Sarika Jha for being readily available for consultation and correction and for running miscellaneous errands. Last but not the least, I thank my wife for bearing with me when I was annoyingly busy with the translations.

Kuldip Salil

1.1.2008

1770, Outram lines,
Kingsway Camp, Delhi-110 009

सूची

मीर तक़ी मीर

हस्ती अपनी हबाब की सी है 20

उल्टी हो गई सब तदबीरें कुछ न दवा ने काम किया 22

जिस सर को ग़रूर आज है यों ताजवरी का 24

पत्ता-पत्ता बूटा-बूटा हाल हमारा जाने है 26

जिन-जिन को था ये इश्क़ का आज़ार मर गए 28

जो इस शोर से 'मीर' रोता रहेगा 30

फ़क़ीराना आए सदा कर चले 32

मुहम्मद रफ़ी 'सौदा'

गुल फेंके हैं औरों की तरफ़ बल्कि समर भी 36

बदला तिरे सितम का कोई तुझसे क्या करे? 38

ख़्वाजा मीर दर्द

तोहमतें चंद अपने ज़िम्मे धर चले 42

हम तुझसे किस हवस की फलक जुस्तजू करें 44

असद उल्लाह ख़ाँ ग़ालिब

हज़ारों ख़्वाहिशें ऐसी, कि हर ख़्वाहिश पे दम निकले 48

कभी नेकी भी उसके जी में गर आ जाए है मुझसे 50

बाज़ीच-ए-अत्फाल है दुनिया, मिरे आगे 52

दिल ही तो है, न संगो-ख़िश्त दर्द से भर न आए क्यों 54

सब कहां-कुछ लाला-ओ-गुल में नुमायां हो गई 56

मुद्दत हुई है यार को मेहमां किए हुए 58

रोने से और इश्क़ में बेबाक़ हो गए 60

किसी को देके दिल कोई नवा संजे-फुगां क्यों हो 62

इब्राहीम ज़ौक

अब तो घबरा के ये कहते हैं कि मर जाएँगे 68

Contents

Meer Taqi Meer
Our life is but a bubble, nothing more 21
All our efforts went unavailing, the medicine had no effect, at all 23
The head that so proudly wears the crown today 25
Every plant and every petal my condition knows 27
All those stricken with love are dead 29
If Meer continues so loudly to weep 31
Like Faqirs we came and gave our call 33
Mohammad Rafi Sauda
Showering flowers on others 37
How can one avenge oneself for your cruel action 39
Khwaja Mir Dard
A few allegations I have earned against my name 43
O heaven, what is it that we can hope from you to get 45
Asad Ullah Khan Ghalib
Thousands of desires, life-consuming and tough 49
If ever she thinks of being to me a little kind 51
This world for me is but a childern's playground 53
It is heart after all, not brick and stone 55
What shapes and forms must lie buried in dust 57
It is ages now that we were by our friend visited 59
We cried in love and opened up further, thus 61
After losing the heart to somebody 63
Ibrahim Mohammad Zauq
Out of sheer frustration, we'll die now we know 69

लायी हयात आए, कज़ा ले चली, चले 70

मोमिन ख़ाँ मोमिन

नावक-अंदाज़ जिधर दीदः-ए-जानाँ होंगे 74

असर उसको ज़रा नहीं होता 76

बहादुर शाह ज़फ़र

न किसी की आँख का नूर हूँ, न किसी के दिल का करार हूँ 80

लगता नहीं है दिल मेरा, उजड़े दियार में 82

दाग़ देहलवी

खातिर से या लिहाज से मैं मान तो गया 86

उज्र आने में भी है और बुलाते भी नहीं 88

अमीर मीनाई

नावक-ए-नाज से मुश्किल है बचाना दिल का 92

मुहम्मद इक़बाल

गेसु-ए-ताबदार को और भी ताबदार कर 96

सितारों से आगे जहाँ और भी हैं 98

ज़माना देखेगा जब मेरे दिल से महशर उठेगा गुफ़्तगू का 100

तराना-ए-हिन्द 102

नया शिवालय 106

साक़ी 110

मजाज़ लख़नवी

आवारा 114

नौजवान ख़ातून से 120

सारा आलम गोश-बर-आवाज़ है 122

इज़्मे ख़िराम लेते हुए आस्मां से हम 124

जुनूने-शौक अब भी कम नहीं है 126

जोश मलीहाबादी

सोज़े-गम दे के मुझे उसने ये इर्शाद किया 130

Life brought us hither, death comes and takes us away, let it be 71

Momin Khan Momin

Whichever way the arrow-shooting eyes of my beloved are bound 75

She is least affected by my grief 77

Bahadur Shah Zafar

Neither am I a source of light to any eye, nor of comfort to any heart 81

I feel so out of place in this desolate, world 83

Daagh Dehlvi

Out of consideration and concession, I trusted you though 87

She invites not and also has objection to coming 89

Amir Meenai

It is indeed difficult to protect your heart against that sharp shooter's art 93

Mohammad Iqbal

Let your shining hair still brighter shine 97

There are worlds beyond, the stars too 99

The world would see when my heart speaks up like a blast 101

The Anthem of Hindustan 103

The New Temple 107

Saqi 111

Majaz Lukhnavi

The Vagabond 115

To a Young Lady 121

The whole world is intently listening 123

Instructed by heaven to go slow 125

Intensity of my love is not less in any way 127

Josh Malihabadi

She declares after making me addicted to sorrow: 131

फ़िक्र ही ठहरी तो दिल को फिक्रे-खूबां क्यों न हो 132
गुंचे! तेरी जिन्दगी पे दिल हिलता है 134
हफ़ीज़ जालंधरी
अभी तो मैं जवान हूँ 138
हम ही में थी न कोई बात याद न तुम को आ सके 144
जिगर मुरादाबादी
मोहब्बत में क्या-क्या मुक़ाम आ रहे हैं 148
दुनिया के सितम याद, न अपनी ही वफ़ा याद 150

इक लफ़्ज-ए-मुहब्बत का अदना यह फ़साना है 152

साक़ी की हर निगाह पे बल खा के पी गया 154
फिराक़ गोरखपुरी
किसी का यूँ तो हुआ कौन उम्र-भर फिर भी 158
छलक के कम न हो ऐसी कोई शराब नहीं 160

सितारों से उलझता जा रहा हूँ 162
सुकूते-शाम मिटाओ, बहुत अँधेरा है 164

कुछ इशारे थे जिन्हें दुनिया समझ बैठे थे हम 166
शाम भी थी धुआँ धुआँ, हुस्न भी था उदास उदास 168

शामे-ग़म कुछ उस निगाहे-नाज़ की बातें करो 170

सर में सौदा भी नहीं, दिल में तमन्ना भी नहीं 172
शकील बदायूनी
ग़म-ए-आशिकी से कह दो रह-ए-आम तक न पहुँचे 176
आज वो भी इश्क़ के मारे नज़र आने लगे 178
फ़ैज़ अहमद फ़ैज़
मुझसे पहली सी मोहब्बत मेरी महबूब न माँग! 182
गर मुझे इसका यकीं हो, मेरे हमदम, मेरे दोस्त! 184
बोल कि लब आज़ाद हैं तेरे 188
कुत्ते 190

If worrying is our destiny 133
Your life is so moving 135
Hafeez Jallandhri
I am youthful still, still I am young 139
There was nothing special in me 145
Jigar Muradabadi
O what stages in love we are going through 149
I remember neither the cruelties of the world nor my own fidelity 151
This word 'love' is nothing more, nothing less, it may be said 153
Tossed over by Saqi's every single glance, I drank 155
Firaq Gorakhpuri
Nobody loves anybody else forever though 159
There is no wine that decreases not when it spills out 161
I am getting tangled with the stars, unwittingly 163
Let the silence of the evening break, for it's very dark 165
What we had thought was the world 167
The evening too was dusky and darkling, and sad and sombre the beautiful one 169
Speak of those imperious eyes, O thou, this sad evening 171
There is no madness in the head though 173
Shakil Badauni
Let not the sorrow of love the common street hit 177
Now even she seems to be love-lorn, 179
Faiz Ahmed Faiz
Ask me not for love, O dear, like before 183
If I were sure of it, my comrade, my friend 185
Speak up 189
Dogs 191

निसार मैं तेरी गलियों पे ऐ वतन, कि जहाँ 192
तन्हाई 196

जाँ निसार अख़्तर

आखिरी मुलाकात 200
हर एक रूह में इक ग़म छिपा लगे है मुझे 206

अख़्तर-उल ईमान

एक सवाल 210
उम्रे-गुरेज़ा के नाम 212

साहिर लुधियानवी

ताजमहल 218
तंग आ चुके हैं कश्मकशे-जिन्दगी से हम 222
जब कभी उनकी तवज्जोह में कमी पाई गई 224
चन्द कलियाँ नशात की चुनकर 226

कैफ़ी आज़मी

सोमनाथ 230
एक लम्हा 232
खारो-ख़स तो उठे, रास्ता तो चले 234

सरदार जाफ़री

सुबहे-फ़रदा 238
मेरा सफ़र 242

मजरूह सुल्तानपुरी

मुझे सहल हो गईं मंजिलें वो हवा के रुख भी बदल गए 248
जब हुआ इरफ़ा तो ग़म आराम-ए-जाँ बनता गया 250

नासिर काज़मी

गए दिनों का सुराग़ लेकर किधर से आया किधर गया वो 254
दयारे-दिल की रात में चिराग़-सा जला गया 256

हरि चन्द अख़्तर

शबाब आया किसी बुत पर फ़िदा होने का वक्त आया 260

Let me bow before you 193
Loneliness 197
Jaan Nisar Akhtar
The Last Meeting 201
Some sorrow or the other is hidden in every heart 207
Akhtar-ul-Iman
A Question 211
To the uncaring life 213
Sahir Ludhianvi
Taj Mahal 219
The struggle and strains of life 223
Whenever I find her attention wandering 225
I pick up some buds of happiness 227
Kaifi Azmi
Somnath 231
A moment 233
Remove bramble and dry grass, let the road be cleared 235
Ali Sardar Jafri
The New Dawn 239
My Journey 243
Majrooh Sultanpuri
Even the wind changed its course and the destination became easy to reach 249
When understanding came 251
Nasir Qazmi
Carrying a clue to the days of yore 255
He lit a candle, so to say, in the night of my heart 257
Hari Chand Akhtar
As I step into my youth 261

'मख़्मूर' देहलवी
किसी से मेरी मंज़िल का पता पाया नहीं जाता 264
'नुशूर' वाहिदी
मैं अभी से किस तरह उनको बेवफ़ा कहूँ 268
अब्दुल हमीद अदम
खाली है अभी जाम, मैं कुछ सोच रहा हूँ 272
मयखाना-ए-हस्ती में अक्सर हम अपना ठिकाना भूल गए 274
क़तील शिफ़ाई
ये मोजिज़ा भी मुहब्बत कभी दिखाए मुझे 278
उस अदा से भी हूँ मैं आशना, तुझे जिस प' इतना ग़रूर है 280

अहमद फ़राज़
रंजिश ही सही, दिल ही दुखाने के लिए आ 284
अब के हम बिछड़े तो शायद कभी ख्वाबों में मिलें 286
अब के ऋुत बदली तो खुशबू का सफर देखेगा कौन 288
परवीन शाकिर
चेहरा मेरा था निगाहें उसकी 292
अब कैसी परदादारी ख़बर आम हो चुकी 294
बारिश हुई तो फूलों के तन चाक हो गए 296

शहरयार
तुम्हारे शहर में कुछ भी हुआ नहीं है क्या 300
तेरे सिवा भी मुझे कोई याद आने वाला था 302

बशीर बद्र
कोई फूल धूप की पत्तियों में हरे रिबन से बँधा हुआ 306
यूँ ही बेसबब न फिरा करो, कोई शाम घर भी रहा करो 308

निदा फ़ाज़ली
दुनिया जिसे कहते हैं, जादू का खिलौना है 312
ख़ुदा ख़ामोश है 314
ऐलान 316
कराची एक माँ है 318

Makhmoor Dehlvi
Nobody can my destination know 265
Nushoor Wahidi
How can I label her unfaithful just yet 269
Abdul Hamid Adam
My cup is empty, yet, and I am lost in thought 273
Often in the tavern, we forgot our place and zone 275
Qateel Shifai
May my love show this miracle too 279
The art of which you are so proud, I know that art too 281
Ahmed Faraz
You may be cross with me 285
Like withered flowers in the books 287
This time, when the season changes 289
Parveen Shakir
The face was mine his the eyes 293
Why hide it, the people already know 295
As it rained, the flowers had holes in their bodies made 297
Shaharyar
Has nothing whatever happened in your city? 301
Apart from you, I had somebody else too in my mind 303
Bashir Badar
Like a flower wrapped in sunlight and tied with a green ribbon 307
Don't be wandering around aimlessly 309
Nida Fazli
This world is a magical toy 313
God is Silent 315
A Declaration 317
Karachi is home to a mother 319

A Treasury of Urdu Poetry

Meer Taqi Meer

(1723-1810)

Meer Taqi Meer is in many ways a pioneer in Urdu poetry. He is easily one of the greatest Urdu poets; some would say he is the greatest. Even Ghalib acknowledged Meer's greatness :

रेख़्ते के तुम्हीं उस्ताद नहीं हो ग़ालिब
कहते हैं अगले ज़माने में कोई मीर भी था

(There was, they say in the olden days a certain Meer too
You alone are not the master, Ghalib of poetry in Urdu).

And another contemporary of Ghalib, Zauq paid him a rare compliment when he said :

न हुआ, न हुआ मीर का अंदाज़ नसीब
ज़ौक यारों ने बहुत ज़ोर ग़ज़ल में मारा

(Others tried their utmost in the field of ghazal, but none could attain the felicity that Meer had).

Meer is essentially a poet of suffering. His poetry is full of grief and sorrow. Apart from the vicissitudes of personal life, the age in which he lived engendered a sombre mood. It was an age of instability, chaos, cruelty and upheaval marked by frequent regime change. Sombre, though Meer's poetry is, it has about it an intensity and authenticity, which gives it universal appeal. He has the rare knack of illustrating and illuminating his observations from ordinary life :

शाम से ही बुझा-सा रहता है
दिल हुआ है चिराग़ मुफ़लिस का

(As the evening approaches, my heart is in a state

of gloom. It is like a poor man's candle).

Meer was born in Agra in the year 1723. His father died when he was only ten or twelve years old. His step-brother who happened to be very jealous of him, gobbled up all parental property. Meer was left high and dry. But extremely self-respecting as he was, he did not approach anybody for help. However a friend of his father gave him five hundred rupees and he was able to tide over the immediate crisis. From Agra, Meer went hunting for work to Delhi and found a job at thirty rupees per month there. But his life knew no peace and stability. Soon, Delhi was attacked by Nadir Shah, and Meer left for Agra, only to come back to Delhi once again. This time he is said to have had an unsuccessful love affair with the daughter of his host, which unhinged him mentally, a state in which he remained for quite some time.

One Sayyad Ali Khan encouraged Meer to write poetry. Very soon Meer established himself in the mushairas (poetic symposia) in Delhi. But perenially disturbed conditions in Delhi made him sick at heart and he decided to leave it. On an invitation from the Nawab of Avadh, he left for Lucknow, where the Nawab received him well. Meer had at last some peace, he was relatively free from financial worries. And he got recognition. In Lucknow, he wrote his two Shikanamas and his autobiography 'Zikre Meer'. He died in 1810 at the ripe old age of 87.

मीर तक़ी मीर

हस्ती अपनी हबाब[1] की सी है
यह नुमाइश सराब[2] की सी है

नाज़ुकी उसके लब की क्या कहिए
पंखड़ी इक गुलाब की सी है

मैं जो बोला कहा कि यह आवाज़
उसी ख़ानाखराब[3] की सी है

बार बार उसके दर प' जाता हूँ
हालत अब इज़्तिराब[4] की सी है

'मीर' उन नीमबाज़[5] आँखों में
सारी मस्ती शराब की सी है।

1. बुलबुला 2. मृगतृष्णा 3. अभागा 4. व्याकुलता 5. अधखुली

Meer Taqi Meer

Our life is but a bubble, nothing more
And this world, is only a mirage at the core

The softness on her lips shows
A red petal on a red rose

As I spoke, immediately said she
This voice must of that wretched man be

Again and again, to her doorstep I go
My mind is infatuated, or nearly so

Meer, these half shut eyes surely link
With intoxication from alcoholic drink

मीर तक़ी मीर

उल्टी हो गई सब तदबीरें कुछ न दवा ने काम किया
देखा! इस बीमारि-ए-दिल ने आखिर काम तमाम किया

अहद-ए-जवानी रो-रो काटा, पीरी में ली आँखें मूँद
यानी रात बहुत थे जागे, सुबह हुई आराम किया

नाहक़ हम मजबूरों पर यह तोहमत है मुख़्तारी की
चाहते हैं सो आप करे हैं हमको अबस[1] बदनाम किया

याँ के सपैद-ओ-सियह में हमको दख़्ल जो है सो इतना है
रात को रो-रो सुबह किया या दिन को जूँ तूँ शाम किया

मीर के दीनो-मज़हब को अब पूछो क्या हो उनने तो
क़श्क़ा[2] खैंचा, दहर[3] में बैठा, कब का तर्क-इस्लाम किया।

1. व्यर्थ, 2. तिलक, 3. मंदिर

Meer Taqi Meer

All our effort went unavailing, the medicine had
no effect at all
This heart-ailment, you can see, has ultimately
ended all

All my youth, I cried and cried, and in old age
closed my eyes
I keep awake all night, so to say, and sleep when
the dawn arrives

Without rhyme or reason, I, the helpless one, am
credited with supremacy
Whatever he likes, he does himself and blames me
unnecessarily

All the power, I have in the affairs here, is only
this much, O
I cry all night till the morning, and see the
morning somehow into the evening go

About Meer's faith and religion, you that would
like to know
He sits in the temple with vermilion on his fore-
head, he gave up Islam long ago

मीर तक़ी मीर

जिस सर को ग़रूर आज है यों ताजवरी का
कल उस प' यहीं शोर है फिर नौहागरी[1] का

आफ़ाक[2] की मंज़िल से गया कौन सलामत
असबाब लुटा राह में याँ हर सफ़री का

जिंदाँ में भी शोरिश[3] न गई अपने जुनूँ की
अब संग मदावा है[4] इस आशुफ्तासरी[5] का

ले साँस भी आहिस्ता कि नाज़ुक है बहुत काम
आफ़ाक़ की इस कारगह-ए-शीशागरी[6] का।

●

---

1. विलाप, 2. संसार, 3. उन्माद, 4. पत्थर ही इलाज है, 5. पागलपन, 6. काँच का सामान बनाने का काम।

Meer Taqi Meer

The head that so proudly wears the crown today
Tomorrow, the cries of mourning will cover it all
the way

No one has gone from this world sound and
square
Every traveller who came, lost his belongings here

Even in prison, my passion lost not its intensity
For this mad head of mine, only the stone can
a cure be

So delicate is the workmanship of this world's glass
factory
That even your breathing here should most gentle
be

मीर तक़ी मीर

पत्ता-पत्ता बूटा-बूटा हाल हमारा जाने है
जाने न जाने गुल ही न जाने बाग़ तो सारा जाने है

चारागरी[1] बीमारि-ए-दिल की रस्म-ए-शहर-ए-हुस्न[2] नहीं
वरना दिलवर नादाँ भी इस दर्द का चारा जाने है

मेहर-ओ-वफा-ओ-लुत्फ-ओ-इनायत[3] एक से वाकिफ इनमें नहीं
और तो सब कुछ तन्ज़-ओ-किनाया[4], रम्ज़-ओ-इशारा जाने है

क्या क्या फ़ितने[5] सर पर उसके लाता है माशूक़ अपना
जिस बेदिल, बेताब-ओ-तर्ब[6] को इश्क का मारा जाने है।

आशिक़-सा तो सादा कोई और न होगा दुनिया में
जी के ज़ियाँ को इश्क़ में उसके अपने वारां जाने है

●

1. इलाज, 2. शहर के हसीनों की परंपरा, 3. कृपा, अनुकंपा, 4. व्यंग्य, संकेत, 5. उपद्रव
6. कटुता सहने वाला।

Meer Taqi Meer

Every plant and every petal my condition knows
Only the flower knows not, the entire garden knows

The cure somebody's heartache is perhaps not the custom in this tinsel town of beauty
My callow beloved too otherwise knows the cure of it surely

Courtesy, mercy, kindness, consistency—she knows none of it
Too well does she know though fling and slant, satire and hit

Only a lovelorn feeble man knows how much heartlessness can sting
And what troubles the beloved one on one's head doth bring

Nobody in the world can be as simple as a lover
When in love, his heart's enemy, his god does he consider

मीर तक़ी मीर

जिन-जिन को था ये इश्क़ का आज़ार मर गए
अक्सर हमारे साथ के बीमार मर गए

यूँ कानों-कान गुल[1] ने न जाना चमन में आह
सर को पटक के हम पसे-दीवार[2] मर गए

सद कारवाँ[3] वफ़ा है कोई पूछता नहीं
गोयां मता-ए-दिल[4] के ख़रीदार मर गए

मजनूं न दश्त[5] में हैं न फ़रहाद कोह[6] में
था जिन से लुत्फ़े ज़िन्दगी वे यार मर गए

घबरा न 'मीर' इश्क़ में इस सलह जीस्त[7] पर
जब बस चला न कुछ तो मेरे यार मर गए

---

1. फूल (प्रियतम) 2. दीवार के पीछे, 3. सैंकड़ों कारखानों में, 4. दिल की दौलत, 5. जंगल, 6. पहाड़, 7. ज़िंदगी।

Meer Taqi Meer

All those stricken with love are dead
Dead all those, who lay beside our bed

Only the blossoms in the garden did not my sighs heed
I died, against the wall breaking my head

Sincerity, even hundredfold, no taker finds,
All those who valued the riches of the heart are dead

Neither is Majnu in the wild, nor Farhad on the hill we find
All those, with whom this life was a joy, have gone ahead

Lose not your heart, O Meer, for these hardships of love
Our friends too, when helpless, chose to be dead

मीर तक़ी मीर

जो इस शोर से 'मीर' रोता रहेगा
तो हमसाया काहे को सोता रहेगा

मुझे काम रोने से अक्सर है नासेह[1]
तू कब तक मिरे मुँह को धोता रहेगा

मिरे दिल ने वो नाला पैदा किया है
जरस[2] के भी जो होश खोता रहेगा

मैं वो रोने वाला चला हूँ जहाँ से
जिसे अब्र हर साल रोता रहेगा

बस ऐ 'मीर' मिज़गाँ[3] से पोंछ आँसुओं को
तू कब तक ये मोती पिरोता रहेगा।

---

1. उपदेशक, 2. घंटा, घड़ियाल, 3. पलक।

Meer Taqi Meer

If Meer continues so loudly to weep
How can his neighbour possibly sleep?

How long will you go on washing my face?
O preacher, I am given to weeping in any case

My heart has given out such a cry
That heaven itself will be puzzled by

I am leaving this world now, but I have been such
a mourner deep
That the clouds will, every year, for me weep

Enough, O Meer, now wipe your tear
How long will you go on weeping, my dear

मीर तक़ी मीर

फ़क़ीराना[1] आए सदा[2] कर चले
मियाँ खुश रहो हम दुआ कर चले

शफ़ा अपनी तक़दीर ही में न थी
कि मक़दूर[3] भर तो दवा कर चले

वो क्या चीज़ है आह जिसके लिए
हर इक चीज़ से दिल उठाकर चले

कोई ना-उमीदाना[4] करते निगाह
सो तुम हमसे मुँह भी छुपाकर चले

दिखाई दिये यूँ कि बेखुद[5] किया
हमें आपसे भी जुदा कर चले

कहें क्या जो पूछे कोई हमसे 'मीर'
जहाँ में तुम आए थे क्या कर चले

---

1. फ़कीरों की तरह, 2. आवाज़ लगाना, 3. ताक़त, 4. निराशापूर्वक, 5. आत्म-विस्मृत।

Meer Taqi Meer

Like faqirs we came and gave our call
May you remain happy, one and all

The cure was just not for us decreed
We tried as much as we could indeed

What is it after all, that could make us
Leave the world for its sake

You should have at least cast a glance, you may
not have obliged
But even your face from me you chose to hide

Your very sight took our bearings away
You sundered us even from ourselves, so to say

What shall we say, Meer, if asked by someone
'You came to the world here, so what have you
done?'

Mohammad Rafi 'Sauda'

(1713-1781)

A contemporary of Meer Taqi Meer, Mirza Mohammad Rafi Sauda was a poetic genius who left his mark practically on every genre of Urdu poetry. The writer of such beautiful couplets as :

किस हस्ती-ए-मोहूम पे नाज़ां है तू ऐ यार
कुछ अपने शबो-रोज़ की है तुझको खबर भी?

(Life that you pride on, O friend, is but an illusion. You have no idea at all as to what the next moment will happen)

wrote, apart from ghazal, qasidas, qatas, satire, masnavi and rubais. He is a poet of rich vocabulary and made significant contribution in the development of Urdu languages. John Gilchrist admires him for enriching the language with fine nuances of expression. He is considered supreme in qasidas, a genre in which his contribution is great indeed. A qasida is a poem generally eulogizing the patron.

Sauda draws freely upon the traditions of Persian poetry. He has a fertile imagination which brings out new patterns of diverse relationships. It creates new perspective and evokes aesthetic response. His ghazals are an expression of various moods. Unlike Meer, he does not indulge in self-pity and pessimism and maintains a healthy outlook on life. His humanism, catholic taste, sincerity of emotion and maturity in thought make his ghazals a vehicle of many-sided sensibility of a period in turmoil.

Sauda was born in 1713 in Delhi. He was employed in the army of Bahadur Shah I. He was a disciple of

Shah Hatim for his Urdu poetry and of Mohammad Zaman for the Persian. He became the poet laureate in 1754. He migrated to Farukhabad in 1771 and from there moved first to Faizabad and then to Lukhnow, where this architect of the Urdu language died in 1781. His poetry is contained in his "Kuliyat" which means the collected works.

मुहम्मद रफ़ी 'सौदा'

गुल फेंके हैं औरों की तरफ़ बल्कि समर[1] भी
ए खानाबरअन्दाज़-ए-चमन[2] कुछ तो इधर भी

क्या ज़िद है मिरे साथ खुदा जानिए वर्ना
काफी है तसल्ली को मिरे एक नज़र भी

किस हस्ति-ए-मौहूम[3] प' नाज़ाँ है[4] तू ऐ यार
कुछ अपने शब-ओ-रोज़ की है तुझको ख़बर भी

तन्हा तिरे मातम में नहीं शाम-ए-सियहपोश[5]
रहता है सदा चाक[6] गरेबान-ए-सहर[7] भी।

---

1. फल, 2. वाटिका को उजाड़ने वाला, 3. भ्रममूलक अस्तित्व, 4. गर्व करता है, 5. कालिमा से लिपटी हुई शाम, 6. फटा हुआ, 7. सुबह

Mohammad Rafi 'Sauda'

Showering flowers on others and giving them fruits too,
Throw something this side also, O destroyer of the garden, you!

Why she is cross with me, I cannot decide,
Otherwise, God knows, with just a glance, I'll be satisfied

The life that you pride on, o friend, is but an illusion
O you have no idea at all as to what the next moment will happen?

Not only is the dark evening for you mourning
The dawn too is ever lamenting

मुहम्मद रफ़ी 'सौदा'

बदला तिरे सितम का कोई तुझसे क्या करे?
अपना ही तू फ़रेफ़्ता[1] होवे खुदा करे

फ़िक्र-ए-मआश[2], इश्क़-ए-बुतां[3], याद-ए-रफ्तगाँ[4]
इस ज़िंदगी में अब कोई क्या-क्या किया करे

गर हो शराब-ओ-ख़लवत-ए-महबूब-ए-खूबरू[5]
ज़ाहिद[6]! तुझे कसम है, जो तू हो तो क्या करे

तन्हा न रोज़-ए-हिज्र ही 'सौदा' पे' है सितम
परवाना-सा विसाल में हर शब जला करे

---

1. आसक्त, 2. जीविका की चिंता, 3. सुंदरियों से प्रेम, 4. बीते दिनों की याद, 5. मदिरा और सुंदर प्रेमिका के साथ एकांत, 6. प्रचारक।

Mohammad Rafi 'Sauda'

How can one avenge oneself for your cruel action
May God, you become a victim of your own
attraction!

Worrying about livelihood, loving the beautiful
ones, reliving the past glory—
How many things can a mortal do in a lifetime
only!

If you have wine and the company of beauties
and solitude too
Tell me honestly, O Zahid, what would you do?

'Sauda' undergoes this anguish not only on days
of separation
But burns like a moth even during union

Khwaja Mir Dard

(1720-1785)

Khwaja Mir Dard who liked to be called Sayyed Khwaja Mir Dard was born in Delhi in 1720. He was son of Mohammad Nassar who was a Persian poet of reputation those days. His uncle too was a poet. Thus, Mir Dard had a family tradition and started writing poetry when he was only fourteen. By the time he was twenty nine he had brought out, 'Vardat-e-Dard'. Apart from the Urdu divan, he produced a book of poems in Persian also.

Mir Dard's poetry has a sharp edge and it is quite effective. He is a poet of serious thought and his poetry is of high quality. Because of their effectiveness, his ghazals remind one of Meer Taqi Meer. These ghazals have seven or nine select couplets. He writes with an intensity and passion. Although his divan is short, it is remarkable in its smoothness and depth of thought. Mir Dard is a poet of philosophical heights and deals with complex problems in his poetry. His diction is select and apt but he has no hesitation in using current idioms. At places, his language can be difficult. But here too the words are so used that they don't hinder our enjoyment of poetry. Some of his couplets have become part of the language:

ज़िंदगी है या कोई तूफान है
हम तो इस जीने के हाथों मर चले
(Is it life or by a storm we are hit
I am simply dying because of it)

Khwaja Mir Dard died in Delhi in 1785.

ख्वाजा मीर दर्द

तोहमतें चंद[1] अपने ज़िम्मे धर चले
किस लिए आए थे हम क्या कर चले

ज़िंदगी है या कोई तूफ़ान है?
हम तो इस जीने के हाथों मर चले

शम्अ की मानिंद हम इस बज़्म में
चश्म-ए-तर[2] आए थे, दामन-तर[3] चले

साक़ियाँ[4] याँ लग रहा है चल-चलाओ
जब तलक बस चल सके साग़र चले

'दर्द'! कुछ मालूम है ये लोग सब
किस तरफ़ से आए थे, किधर चले?

---

1. दो-चार, 2. आँसू बहाते हुए, 3. दामन भिगोए, 4. ऐ साक़ी।

Khwaja Mir Dard

A few allegations I have earned against my name
O what I have done and what for I came!

Is it life or by a storm we are hit
I am simply dying because of it

With our eyes, wet like a candle, to the world we came
And drenched all over, we are leaving the game

Everybody is on the move here, O Saqi
As long as possible, please let the chalice in rotation be

O Dard, do you have any idea from which direction
These people came and which way are they heading?

ख्वाजा मीर दर्द

हम तुझसे किस हवस[1] की फलक[2] जुस्तजू[3] करें।
दिल ही नहीं रहा है जो कुछ आरज़ू करें॥

ना गुल को है सबात[4] ना हमको एतिबार।
किस बात पे चमन हवसे-रंगो-बू करें॥

हर चन्द आईना हूँ पर इतना हूँ नाक़ुबूल[5]
मुँह फेर ले वो, जिसके मुझे रूबरू करें॥

सर-ता-क़दम ज़बान हैं जू शम्मा गो कि हम
पर ये कहाँ मजाल कि कुछ गुफ्तगू करें।

---

1. कामना, 2. आकाश, 3. तलाश, 4. स्थायित्व, 5. अस्वीकार्य

Khwaja Mir Dard

O heaven, what is it that we can hope from you
to get
When the heart itself is missing, what can we
possibly expect!

Neither can I trust myself, nor will this flower be
for long found
For colour and fragrance then, I should hope on
what ground!

I am a mirror, surely, but in such disgrace
That whoever looks at me, turns away his face

Like a lit-up candle, I can speak from every part
But to utter a word here, I dare not

Asad Ullah Khan 'Ghalib'

(1797-1869)

Ghalib is undoubtedly the greatest Urdu poet and one of the greatest in any language. He belonged to a family of Turkish origin. Ghalib was born in Agra in 1797. His father died when he was only five and the family had to be dependant on his maternal grandparents. This position of dependence was prolonged by his marriage at the age of thirteen in Delhi. Once in Delhi, Ghalib became a part of the sophisticated circle and started living in their style. He had a good grounding in logic, astronomy, metaphysics and medicine. If anyone could be called his teacher, it was the Persian and Arabic scholar Abdul Samad. Otherwise, he was self-taught in the art of poetry. Ghalib fell in love with a dancing girl and nothing inspires his poetic impulse as she does in her various moods of cruelty, sorrow and coquettery.

Delhi, for all its disturbed conditions, had a good atmosphere for poetry. Determined to be a poet of distinction, he started writing poetry in an original and difficult style. But under the advice of his friend Fazal-e-Haq, he tried to write in a more intelligible language. Ghalib lived beyond his means. As a result he borrowed heavily and when he was not able to repay, he was sentenced. Also, he had to undergo a jail term for gambling. After the revolt of 1857, Ghalib felt very lonely and sad. In his last years, his health deteriorated and he died in 1869.

Ghalib is a very witty poet who can laugh not only on others but also at himself. His sense of humour sustains him in the midst of misfortunes and tragedies that befell him. If, on the one hand, he writes "But a king's courtier, he struts up and down, otherwise who cares for Ghalib in the town",

on the other, he asks,

"What business of life without Ghalib, the wretched
has shut its door
W..y cry your heart out if he is no more"

Ghalib was a great poet who did not get his due in his lifetime. In fact he was ahead of his times, and he knew it. He also knew that the future generations will recongize his greatness. And he was right.

Great poets are prophets indeed.

हज़ारों ख़्वाहिशें ऐसी, कि हर ख़्वाहिश पे दम निकले।
बहुत निकले मिरे अरमान लेकिन फिर भी कम निकले।

निकलना खुल्द[1] से आदम का सुनते आए थे लेकिन
बहुत बेआबरू होकर तेरे कूचे से हम निकले

हुई जिनसे तवक़्क़ो, खस्तगी[2] में दाद पाने की
वो हमसे भी ज़्यादा कुश्ता-ए-तेग़े-सितम[3] निकले

मुहब्बत में नहीं है फ़र्क़, जीने और मरने में
उसी को देखकर जीते हैं जिस काफ़िर पे दम निकले

खुदा के वास्ते पर्दा न काबे से उठा ज़ालिम
कहीं ऐसा न हो यां भी वही काफ़िर सनम निकले

कहाँ मैखाने का दरवाज़ा, 'ग़ालिब' और कहाँ वाइज़
पर इतना जानते हैं कल वो जाता था कि हम निकले

---

1. स्वर्ग, 2. पागलपन, 3. अत्याचार का मारा हुआ

'Ghalib'

Thousands of desires, life-consuming and tough
I had them fulfilled in plenty, but not enough

Expulsion of man from paradise we had known
But how disgracefully from your street we've been
thrown

The people who we thought, would commiserate
with us in distress
Themselves turned out to be more oppressed, not
less

In love, there is no difference between life and
death
We die for the same infidel who's our life's breath

For heaven's sake, do not open the door of Kaba,
lest there too I should see
The same infidel, looking at me bewitchingly

Is there any relation between the door of tavern
and the preacher, please say
But believe me, as I was coming out, he was going
in yesterday

'ग़ालिब'

कभी नेकी भी उसके जी में गर आ जाए है मुझसे
जफ़ाएं करके अपनी याद शर्मा जाए है मुझसे

खुदाया, जज़्ब-ए-दिल की मगर तासीर उल्टी है
कि जितना खेंचता हूँ उतना खिंचता जाये है मुझसे

उधर वो बदगुमानी है, इधर यह नातवानी[1] है
न पूछा जाये है उससे, न बोला जाये है मुझसे

संभलने दे मुझे, ऐ नाउम्मीदी, क्या क़यामत है
कि दामाने-खयाले-यार[2], छूटा जाये है मुझसे

हुए हैं पाँव ही पहले नबर्दे-इश्क[3] में ज़ख्मी
न भागा जाए है मुझसे, न ठहरा जाए है मुझसे

क़यामत है, कि होवे मुद्दई का हमसफर, 'ग़ालिब'
वो काफ़िर, जो खुदा को भी न सौंपा जाए है मुझसे

1. निर्बलता, 2. मित्र की कल्पना का दामन, 3. प्रेम का संघर्ष।

'Ghalib'

If ever she thinks of being to me a little kind
She's abashed as her cruelties cross her mind

The desire of my heart, O God, has but a contrary
effect
More she goes away from me, as more I try to
attract

There, it is such arrogance, such feebleness here
That neither can I speak, nor will she enquire my
welfare

Let me hold myself together, O despair
O damn it, I cannot hold on to the thought of
a friend fair

Because of wandering in love, my feet are just
undone
I neither can stay put nor can I run

O misery, that she should with my rival be
She, whom, O Ghalib, even with God I cannot
see

बाज़ीच-ए-अत्फ़ाल[1] है दुनिया, मिरे आगे
होता है शबो रोज़ तमाशा, मिरे आगे

इक खेल है औरंगे-सुलेमां[2], मिरे नज़दीक
इक बात है, ऐजाज़े - मसीहा[3], मिरे आगे

होता है निहां गर्द में सहरा, मिरे होते
घिसता है जबीं[4] ख़ाक पे दरिया मिरे आगे

मत पूछ, कि क्या हाल है मेरा, तिरे पीछे
तू देख, कि क्या रंग है तेरा, मिरे आगे

ईमां मुझे रोके है, तो खेंचे है मुझे कुफ्र
काबा मिरे पीछे है, कलीसा[5] मिरे आगे

खुश होते हैं पर वस्ल में यूं मर नहीं जाते
आई शबे-हिजरां[6] की तमन्ना मिरे आगे

गो हाथ को जुम्बिश नहीं, आँखों में तो दम है
रहने दो अभी साग़र - ओ - मीना मिरे आगे

हम पेश-ओ-हम मशरब-ओ-हम राज़[7] है मेरा।
'ग़ालिब' को बुरा क्यों, कहो अच्छा, मिरे आगे

---

1. बच्चों का खेल, 2. सुलेमान का राजसिंहासन, 3. ईसा का चमत्कार (ईसा की फूँक से मुर्दे ज़ी उठते थे), 4. माथा, 5. गिरजाघर, 6. विरह यामिनी, 7. सहव्यवसायी; सहपंथी

'Ghalib'

This world for me is but a children's playground
Where day and night a funny something is
happening around

Solomon's throne for me is only a plaything
And Christ's miracle an ordinary something

Under the dust raised by me, I see a desert hidden
around
And the river before me rubs its forehead on the
ground

Ask me not how I fare in your absence
But see how you look in my presence

Truth pulls at me, as falsehood attractive I find
The cathedral is in my front, the Kaba behind

Be happy on meeting, but go not overboard prithee
I am haunted by the joys of separation already

My hands are lifeless though, my eyes are still bright
Remove not the cup and the bottle yet from my sight

Ghalib is a colleague, co-professional and a comrade
Call him good before me, rather than degrade

'ग़ालिब'

दिल ही तो है, न संगो-ख़िश्त[1] दर्द से भर न आए क्यों
रोयेंगे हम हज़ार बार, कोई हमें सताए क्यों

दैर नहीं, हरम नहीं, दर नहीं, आस्तां नहीं
बैठे हैं रहगुज़र पे हम, कोई हमें उठाए क्यों

जब वो जमाले-दिल-फरोज़[2] सूरते-मेहरे-नीमरोज़[3]
आप ही हों नज़ारा सोज़, पर्दे में मुँह छिपाए क्यों

क़ैदे-हयातो-बंदे-ग़म[4], अस्ल में दोनों एक हैं
मौत से पहले, आदमी ग़म से नजात पाए क्यों

वां वो ग़ुरूरे-इज्जों-नाज[5] यां यह हिजाबे-पास-वज़्अ[6]
राह में हम मिलें कहाँ, बज़्म में वो बुलाए क्यों

हां वो नहीं खुदा परस्त, जाओ वो बेवफ़ा सही
जिसको हो दीनो-दिल अज़ीज़, उसकी गली में जाए क्यों

'ग़ालिबे'-खस्ता[7] के बिग़ैर कौन से काम बंद हैं
रोइए ज़ार ज़ार[8] क्या, कीजिए हाय हाय क्यों

---

1. ईंट-पत्थर, 2. मन को प्रकाशित करने वाला रूप, 3. दोपहर के सूर्य की भाँति, 4. जीवन-कारा और दुख बंधन, 5. अपनी शान का गर्व, 6. अपनी व्यवहार प्रणाली को न बदलने का संकोच, 7. दुर्दशाग्रस्त गालिब, 8. फूट-फूट कर।

'Ghalib'

It is heart after all, not brick and stone, why won't
it well up with pain,
Why should anybody harass us, we shall a thou-
sand times cry

No home, no hearth for us, no temple, no mosque
Why should anybody remove us from the thorough-
fare, can we ask?

Her beauty illumines all, a full waxing moon in
grace
Loveliness incarnate indeed, why should she hide
her face

Life's incarceration and bondage to suffering are the
same thing indeed
Until our death how can we from suffering be
relieved

He is puffed up with status high, and we have
to keep our self-respect right
How can we meet half way, why would he to
his gathering invite

Alright, he is not kindhearted, nor faithful he, so
Why should anybody who loves his faith and life,
to his street go

What business of life, without Ghalib the miserable,
has shut its door
Why should anybody cry his heart out if he's no
more

'ग़ालिब'

सब कहां-कुछ लाल-ओ-गुल[1] में नुमायां[2] हो गईं
ख़ाक में क्या सूरतें होंगी, कि पिन्हाँ हो गईं

इन परीज़ादों[3] से लेंगे ख़ुल्द में हम इन्तिक़ाम
कुदरते-हक़ से, यही हूरें अगर वाँ हो गईं

नींद उसकी है, दिमाग उसका है, रातें उसकी हैं
तेरी ज़ुल्फ़ें, जिसके बाज़ू पर, परीशाँ हो गईं

मैं चमन में क्या गया, गोया दबिस्ताँ[4] खुल गया
बुलबुलें सुन कर मिरे नाले, ग़ज़लख़्वाँ[5] हो गईं

वो निगाहें, क्यों हुई जाती हैं, यारब दिल के पार
जो मिरी कोताहि-ए-क़िस्मत[6] से मिशगाँ हो गईं

वाँ गया भी मैं, तो उनकी गालियों का क्या जवाब
याद थी जितनी दुआएँ, सर्फ़े-दरबाँ हो गईं

रंज से खूगर[7] हुआ इंसाँ, तो मिट जाता है रंज
मुश्किलें मुझ पर पड़ी इतनी कि आसाँ हो गईं

यूँ ही गर रोता रहा 'गालिब', तो ऐ अहले-जहाँ[8]
देखना इन बस्तियों को तुम, कि वीराँ हो गईं

---

1. गुलाब के फूल, 2. प्रकट, 3. परी, 4. पाठशाला, 5. गजल गाने वाला, 6. बदकिस्मती, 7. अभ्यस्त, 8. दुनिया वालो।

'Ghalib'

What shapes and forms must lie buried in dust
Not all, but only a few in the form of flowers burst

If by some miracle they can do that place make
In heaven, surely we'll on the beauties our revenge take

The nights are really his, his is the sleep, he alone can proud be
On whose arms you allow your tresses to flow free

As I went to the garden, it began with verse and melody to ring
For, the nightingales, as they heard my cries, began to sing

Why are these eyes, God, piercing my heart through
Which only because of my bad luck into her eyebrows grew

What possibly, will now my response to her abuses be
For, I have expended all the prayers I knew to the doorkeeper already

Once you get used to sorrow, sorrow it ceases to be
So many hardships befell me that they became easy

If Ghalib keeps weeping like this, O people of the world
You will soon see these towns into wilderness hurled

'ग़ालिब'

मुद्दत हुई है यार को मेहमां किए हुए
जोशे-क़दह[1] से, बज़्म चरागाँ किए हुए

दिल फिर तवाफे-कू-ए-मलामत[2] को जाए है
पिन्दार[3] का सनमकदा वीराँ किए हुए

फिर शौक कर रहा है खरीददार को तलब
अर्जे-मता-ए-अक़्ल-ओ-दिल-ओ-जाँ[4] किए हुए

माँगे है फिर, किसी को लबे-बाम[5] पर, हवस
जुल्फे-सियाह रुख पे परीशाँ किए हुए

इक नौबहारे-नाज[6] को ताके है फिर, निगाह
चेहरा फ़रोगे-मै[7] से गुलिस्ताँ किए हुए

फिर, जी में है कि दर पे किसी के पड़े रहें
सर ज़ेरे - बारे - मिन्नते - दरबाँ[8] किए हुए

जी ढूँढ़ता है फिर वही फुर्सत, कि रात दिन
बैठे रहें तसव्वुरे - जानाँ[9] किए हुए

---

1. मदिरा का उबाल, 2. धिक्कार की गली की परिक्रमा, 3. घमण्ड, 4. दिलों-जाँ की दौलत 5. छज्जे पर, 6. सौन्दर्याभिमान की नई बहार में डूबा हुआ आकार, नवयौवन के रंगों से लहलहाता रूप, 7. मदिरा की आभा, 8. दरबान, 9. माशूक की कल्पना।

'Ghalib'

It is ages now that we were by our friend visited
And had the house with cups of wine illuminated

To the winds, once again, all my ego throwing
I feel like to that street of my infamy going

For my heart, my soul and the mind
My love would fain a customer find

Her black tresses spread all around her face
My passion once again wants somebody on the
terrace

With her face all flush and blooming with wine
A fresh coquettish beauty is the wish of these eyes
of mine

My head, out of gratitude to the gatekeeper
crawling
Once again, I feel like on her doorstep sprawling

To keep sitting, wrapped in thoughts of the beloved
sleek
Once again, those days and nights of leisure doth
the heart seek

'ग़ालिब'

रोने से और इश्क़ में बेबाक[1] हो गए
धोए गए हम ऐसे कि बस पाक हो गए

रुस्वा-ए-दहर[2] गो हुए, आवारगी से तुम
बारे तबीअतों के तो चालाक हो गए

कहता है कौन नाला-ए-बुलबुल[3] को, बे असर
परदे में गुल के लाख जिगर चाक हो गए

पूछे है क्या वुजूद-ओ-अदम[4] अहले-शौक़ का
आप अपनी आग से खस-ओ-खाशाक[5] हो गए

करने गए थे उससे, तग़ाफ़ुल का हम गिला
की एक ही निगाह, कि बस खाक हो गए

इस रंग से उठाई कल उसने 'असद' की लाश
दुश्मन भी जिसको देख के ग़मनाक[6] हो गए

1. खुल, 2. संसार भर में अपमानित, 3. बुलबुल का आर्तनाद, 4. अस्तित्व और अनस्तित्व, 5. कूड़ा-करकट, 6. दुःखी

'Ghalib'

We cried in love and opened up further, thus
So well we were washed that it cleansed us

You may have become a butt of ridicule because of
the wander-itch
It has certainly made you smart and experience -
rich

Who says the cries of the nightingale unavailing
went
Beneath the flower's body, a thousand hearts were
rent

Of the life and death of a lover, O ask not
In their own fire they have been to cinders
wrought

I had gone to her to complain of her indifference
worst
But a single look from her reduced me to dust

She so lifted 'Asad's' corpse yesterday
That even his enemies could not their tears stay

'ग़ालिब'

किसी को देके दिल कोई नवा संजे-फुगाँ क्यों हो
न हो जब दिल ही सीने में, तो फिर मुँह में ज़ुबाँ क्यों हो

किया ग़मख़्वार ने रुस्वा, लगे आग इस मुहब्बत को
न लावे ताब जो ग़म की, वो मेरा राज़दाँ क्यों हो

वो अपनी खू न छोड़ेंगे, हम अपनी वज़्अ क्यों बदलें
सुबुकसर[1] बन के क्या पूछें कि हमसे सरगिरां[2] क्यों हो

दफ़ा कैसी, कहाँ का इश्क़, जब सर फोड़ना ठहरा
तो फिर, ऐ संग दिल, तेरा ही संगे-आस्ताँ क्यों हो

क़फस[3] में, मुझसे, रुदादे-चमन[4] कहते, न डर, हमदम
गिरी है जिस पे कल बिजली, वो मेरा आशियाँ[5] क्यों हो

यह फितना, आदमी की खाना-वीरानी को क्या कम है
हुए तुम दोस्त जिसके, दुश्मन उसका आस्माँ क्यों हो

'Ghalib'

After losing the heart to somebody, why should
one grumble and sigh
When there is no heart in the breast, why should
the tongue in the mouth lie

Damned be this love, my friend annoyed I see
If he cannot bear with my grief, how can he a
friend be

She will not change his attitude, then why should
my ways be changed
Why humiliate myself, and ask him why she is
estranged

What fealty, what love, if I have to break my head
against a stone
And then, O stone-hearted one, why should it be
your door-step alone

Fear not, and the garden's tale to me in the prison
freely say
Why should it belong to me, the nest hit by the
lightning yesterday

To what misery won't this misfortune lead
With you as a friend, why should one an enemy
need

यही है आज़माना, तो सताना किसको कहते हैं
उदू[6] के हो लिए जब तुम, तो मेरा इम्तिहाँ क्यों हो

निकाला चाहता है काम क्या तानों से तू, 'गालिब'
तेरे बेमेह्र[7] कहने से, वो तुझ पर मेहरबाँ क्यों हो

---

1. अपमानित, 2. अप्रसन्न, 3. पिंजरा, 4. उद्यान का हाल, 5. नीड़, 6. शत्रु, 7. प्रेमविहीन।

If this is testing, then what's torturing?
If you are for my foe, then why me are you testing

Ghalib, what purpose would it serve, that you taunt
her, as you do
Do you think, if you call her unkind, she will be
kind to you

Ibrahim Mohammad Zauq

(1789-1854)

Some of the best-known poets of the Urdu language congregated at the court of Bahadur Shah Zafar. Zauq was not only one of them, he was also the ustad (teacher) of the emperor. Zauq was born in Delhi in 1789. His father had come here from Muzaffarnagar (U.P.) in search of livelihood. Zauq had his early education in elementary Persian and the holy Quran at a maktab (religious school) run by Sheikh Mohammad Ramzan, who also corrected Zauq's early poems. Later Zauq turned to Shah Nazir to learn the art of poetry. He was introduced to Zafar, who was then the crown prince, by a friend. Zauq was a gifted poet and was more popular in his time than his illustrious contemporaries like Ghalib and Momin. He was a good-natured person, gentle in behaviour, soft spoken and devoted to poetry.

Zauq is considered the greatest writer of qasida (poem of praise) after Sauda. He wrote a qasida and presented it at the court of Akbar Shah II for which he was given the title of 'Khaqaini-e-Hind'. In fact he wrote a qasida for every auspicious occasion. He had left behind a school of poetry, further developed by Daagh Dehlvi who, as also Mohammad Hussain Azad, was his disciple. Zauq is a poet of sweet diction and simple language.

It is believed that there was some rivalry between Zauq and Ghalib, which led Ghalib to write his masterly couplet

बना है शह का मुसाहिब फिरे है इतराता
वगरना शहर में ग़ालिब की आबरू क्या है

(But a king's courtier, he struts up and down
Otherwise who cares for Ghalib (actually Zauq) in
the town)

Ghalib was a great master of satire, but that does not detract from Zauq's importance as a poet. How many poets can write a more moving, profound and memorable couplet than this :

लाई हयात, आये, कज़ा ले चली, चले
अपनी खुशी न आये न अपनी खुशी चले

(Life brought us hither, death comes and takes us
away, let it be
We came neither on our own volition, nor go from
here out of choice free)

After prolonged illness, Zauq died in 1854. Zauq did not care to publish his poetry in his lifetime, which was published posthumously by his disciples and other lovers of poetry.

इब्राहीम ज़ौक

अब तो घबरा के ये कहते हैं कि मर जाएँगे
मरके भी चैन न पाया तो किधर जाएँगे

आग दोज़ख़ की भी हो जाएगी पानी-पानी
जब ये आँसी[1] 'अर्के-शरम'[2] से तर जाएँगे

हम नहीं वो जो करें खून का दावा तुम पर
बल्कि पूछेगा खुदा भी तो मुकर जाएँगे

रुख़े-रोशन से नक़ाब अपने उलट देखो तुम
महरो-माह[3]-नज़रों से यारों की उतर जाएँगे

ज़ौक जो मदरसे के हैं बिगड़े हुए मुल्ला
उनको मैखाने में ले आओ, सँवर जाएँगे

---

1. पापी, 2. लज्जा का पसीना, 3. चाँद-सूरज

Ibrahim Zauq

Out of sheer frustration, we'll die now, we know
But after death also, if we don't get peace, where
do ,we go?

Hell-fires too are going to be cold and wet
When these sinners in repentance sweat

We are not the ones to accuse you of our
assasination
On the contrary, even if God says so, will refute
the allegation

You have only to remove the veil from your lovely
face and see
How the sun and the moon lose their luster entirely

Zauq, the mullahs, who because of the madarsas
have gone astray
Bring them to the tavern and they will find their
way

इब्राहीम ज़ौक

लायी हयात[1] आए, कज़ा ले चली, चले
अपनी खुशी न आए न अपनी खुशी चले

बेहतर तो है यही कि न दुनिया से दिल लगे
पर क्या करें जो काम न बे दिल-लगी चले

कम होंगे इस बिसात[2] पे हम जैसे बद-किमार[3]
जो चाल हम चले सो निहायत बुरी चले

दुनिया ने किस का राहे-फ़ना में दिया है साथ
तुम भी चले चलो यूँ ही जब तक चली चले

नाज़ाँ न हो खिरद[4] पे जो होना है वो ही हो
दानिश तेरी न कुछ मेरी दानिशवरी[5] चले।

---

1. ज़िन्दगी, 2. ज़मीन पर बिछाने का कपड़ा (यहाँ जुए की फड़ से तात्पर्य है), 3. जुआरी, 4. बुद्धि, 5. समझदारी।

Ibrahim Zauq

Life brought us hither, death comes and takes us away, let it be
We came neither on our own volition, nor go from here out of choice free

Better it is if we are not in the attractions of the world trapped
But what do we do if it is not possible to live unattached

Hardly a gambler like us could this chess-board have had
Every move we made, was extremely bad

Who can go with you on your journey after death, O man
You should also carry on in this world as long as you can

Be not proud of your intelligence, take it that what happens is fine
For, in this, neither your wisdom can help nor mine

Momin Khan Momin

(1801-1852)

It is said that when Ghalib read the following couplet:

तुम मेरे पास होते हो गोया
जब कोई दूसरा नहीं होता

(You are by my side
When there is none other beside)

he was so impressed that he offered to barter away his whole divan for this one couplet. Momin, the story goes, contemptuously rejected the offer. Now, we all know that Momin is no match for Ghalib. He is however, at places very good. Some of his ghazals are very famous. For instance :

वो जो हम में तुम में करार था तुम्हें याद हो कि न याद हो
वो ही वादा यानी निबाद का तुम्हें याद हो कि न याद हो

(You may or may not remember now that once we loved each other and had decided to remain in love).

And this ghazal :

रोया करेंगे आप भी पहरों इसी तरह
अटका कहीं जो आपका दिल भी मेरी तरह

(If ever you are caught in somebody's love
You will also cry as I am crying for you now).

Like that of all poets who live after their times, Momin's poetry has individuality. He has his own style of expression. Living for just fifty one years, Hakim Momin Khan Momin was born in 1801. His father had migrated from Kashmir and received a pension from East India Company. Momin studied Indian medicine, but did not do regular practice. He was interested in astrology and classical music also, and was fond of chess too. He was a great Don Juan who had love affair with many ladies. And he narrates his love stories with great relish and brutality. Momin's "Complete works" (Kuliyat) were compiled in 1843 and published a little later. A Persian divan appeared in 1854 after his death. He died in 1852. The story goes that Momin had predicted his death.

मोमिन खाँ मोमिन

नावक-अंदाज़[1] जिधर दीदः-ए-जानाँ[2] होंगे
नीम बिस्मिल[3] कई होंगे कई बे-जाँ होंगे

ताब-ए-नज़्ज़ारा[4] नहीं, आइना क्या देखने दूँ
और बन जाएँगे तसवीर जो हैरां होंगे

तू कहाँ जाएगी कुछ अपना ठिकाना कर ले
हम तो कल ख़्वाब-ए-आदम[5] में शब-ए-हिज्राँ[6] होंगे

एक हम हैं कि हुए ऐसे पशेमान कि बस
एक वो हैं कि जिन्हें चाह के अरमां होंगे

उम्र तो सारी कटी इश्क़-ए-बुताँ में 'मोमिन'
आखिरी वक़्त में क्या ख़ाक मुसलमाँ होंगे?

---

1. तीर चलाने वाला, 2. प्रेमिका की दृष्टि, 3. घायल, 4. देखने की शक्ति, 5. चिरनिद्रा, 6. विरह की रात।

Momin Khan Momin

Whichever way the arrow-shooting eyes of my
beloved are bound
Many a one will be wounded, many a one lifeless
found

She will not be able to stand it, and I must not
let her into the mirror see
Into a wall painting she'll turn astonished at her
own beauty

Think of some other abode, O evening of
separation, O where will you go
For, I'll be lying in eternal sleep by tomorrow

Here, we are, who with repentance burn
While there are others who for love still yearn

All my life, I have worshipped one or the other
human form
It is too late for me now, O Momin, to turn to
Islam

मोमिन खाँ मोमिन

असर उसको ज़रा नहीं होता
रंज राहत-फ़िज़ा[1] नहीं होता

तुम हमारे किसी तरह न हुए
वर्ना दुनिया में क्या नहीं होता

उसने क्या जाने क्या किया लेकर
दिल किसी काम का नहीं होता

तुम मिरे पास होते हो गोया
जब कोई दूसरा नहीं होता

हाल-ए-दिल यार को लिखूँ क्योंकर
हाथ दिल से जुदा नहीं होता

चारः-ए-दिल सिवाय सब्र नहीं
सो तुम्हारे सिवा नहीं होता

क्यों सुने अर्ज़-ए-मुज़तर[2] ऐ 'मोमिन'
सनम[3] आखिर खुदा नहीं होता

---

1. शांति और सुख बढ़ाने वाला, 2. व्याकुल की प्रार्थना, 3. मूर्ति, प्रेमिका।

Momin Khan Momin

She is least affected by my grief
I hardly get any relief

I could never claim you for mine
Otherwise, the world would have been just fine

I don't know what for she took my heart away
It was of no use, in any way

You are always by my side
When there is nobody else beside

How can I write my heart's condition to my love
When my hand from my heart I cannot remove

Only in patience lies my peace of mind
Which without you I cannot find

How would she hear, O Momin, the prayer of
man in misery
The beloved is not after all a god of mercy

Bahadur Shah Zafar

(1775-1862)

The writer of such immortal couplets as :

कितना है बदनसीब ज़फ़र दफ़न के लिये
दो गज़ ज़मीन भी न मिली कूए-यार में

(How unfortunate, Zafar did not get
Even two yards of land for burial in his beloved's (India) lane)

Or

यह चमन यूं ही रहेगा और हज़ारों जानवर
अपनी-अपनी बोलियाँ सब बोलकर उड़ जायेंगे

(This garden will remain as it is, while thousands of birds will come and fly out of here after singing their respective songs).

Bahadur Shah Zafar whose full name is Siraj-u-din. Mohammad Bahadur Shah Zafar was the last Mughal Emperor who led India's first war of independence against the British. His poetry is a cry straight from the heart; it is a cry born out of deep anguish and utter helplessness. He was a prolific writer who wrote four volumes of poetry. He is not as great a poet as his illustrious contemporaries like Zauq and Ghalib. But his ghazals show dexterity in the use of rhyme and word-play. He uses idiomatic language close to the language of the common man. In this sense, he is an accomplished poet. Zafar was a disciple of Naseer and Zauq and later, after Zauq's death, that of Ghalib.

Although he was an emperor, he was temperamentally unfit to rule. Poetry, which depends on the dictates of the heart, and running an empire which requires ruthlessness, hardly go together. Hence Zafar is a poet of grief and sorrow, and even self-pity. His poetry reveals a stoic and mystical personality with a deep concern for moral values while he himself goes through deep despair and acute sufferings. He seems to regard humility and acceptance of one's fate as great human virtues. He refrains from ornamentation and concentrates on musicality in his ghazals. There is in his poetry not much conventional yearning for the beloved. His poetry is an aesthetic self-expression of a stoic who looks for life's vision in sufferings. Bahadur Shah also wrote some haunting and melodious geets. He invented some new radif patterns in his ghazals. All in all, he is not among the greats of Urdu poetry, but some of his ghazals are among the greatest. Zafar died in Rangoon in the year 1862.

बहादुर शाह ज़फ़र

न किसी की आँख का नूर हूँ, न किसी के दिल का क़रार हूँ।
जो किसी के काम न आ सके मैं वो एक मुश्ते-गुबार[1] हूँ॥

मेरा रंग रूप बिगड़ गया, मेरा यार मुझसे बिछड़ गया।
जो चमन ख़िज़ाँ से उजड़ गया मैं उसी की फ़स्ले-बहार हूँ॥

पढ़े फ़ातेहा कोई आए क्यों, कोई चार फूल चढ़ाए क्यों।
कोई आके शम्मअ जलाए क्यों, मैं वो बेकसी का मज़ार हूँ॥

मैं नहीं हूँ नग़्मा-ए-जांफ़िज़ा, मुझे सुन के कोई करेगा क्या।
मैं बड़े बियोग की हूँ सदा, मैं बड़े दुखों की पुकार हूँ॥

---

1. मुट्ठी भर खाक

Bahadur Shah Zafar

Neither am I a source of light to any eye, nor of
comfort to any heart
I am only a handful of dust, of no use of any
sort

My friends from me are separated, my looks and
lustre are lost
I am the remnant of a garden, ruined in the autumn
past

Why should anybody come and pray here, why
should anybody flowers place
Why should anybody light a candle on a tomb
in such disgrace

I am not a life-giving song that one should come
and hear
I am a song of parting instead, a song of sorrow
and care

बहादुर शाह ज़फ़र

लगता नहीं है दिल मेरा, उजड़े दियार[1] में।
किसकी बनी है आलमे-नापायदार[2] में॥

कह दो इन हसरतों से, कहीं और जा बसें।
इतनी जगह कहाँ है दिले-दाग़दार[3] में॥

उम्रे-दराज़[4] माँगकर, लाए थे चार दिन।
दो आरज़ू में कट गए, दो इन्तिज़ार में॥

कितना है बदनसीब 'ज़फ़र' दफ़न के लिए।
दो गज़ ज़मीन भी न मिली कूए-यार[5] में॥

---

1. देश, 2. नश्वर, 3. दागदार हृदय, 4. लम्बी आयु, 5. प्रेमिका की गली (देश में)

Bahadur Shah Zafar

I feel so out of place in this desolate, in this unstable
world
Of anybody having a smooth sailing here, I have
never heard

They should go and reside somewhere else, tell
these yearnings,
My scarred heart has no room left for such things

Of this gift of a 'long life' of four days' lasting
Two have gone in yearning, two in waiting

Not to have got even two yards of land in his
beloved's lane,
How unfortunate in burial doth Zafar remain!

Daagh Dehlvi

(1831-1905)

Perhaps no other poet has had a larger number of disciples than Daagh, whose full name was Nawab Mirza Daagh Dehlvi. Among his disciples was no less a person than Mohammad Iqbal, who sent him his compositions by post. Daagh was born in 1831. He was the son of famous Shamas Din Ahmed of Ferozepur Jhirka who was executed by the British for plotting the murder of the resident of Delhi. After the death of his father, Daagh went to Rampur and then came to Delhi. He moved over to Rampur again following the revolt of 1857. He settled there under the patronage of three successive Nawabs. Daagh is best known for the kind of language he employed in poetry. It is a simple and chaste Urdu; it is very lucid. And his poetry is highly sensuous. It is this lucidity of diction and the sensuousness of experience that attracted large number of poets to write in his manner. He was a disciple of Zauq. To use a cliché, Daagh was indeed an institution.

However, much as one may admire Daagh's style and mastery of spoken idiom, he cannot be counted among the greats of Urdu poetry. At places, he is shallow, even frivolous. And very often he lacks the profundity of, say, a Ghalib or Iqbal or the vision of a Faiz Ahmed Faiz. Eliot's comment that one enjoys Shelley's poetry till the age of fifteen, even though a little discourteous, is perhaps not too wrong when applied to Daagh. All the same, if not great, Daagh is a significant poet.

After twenty four years' stay in Rampur, Daagh went

had and became a court poet. Among his works
e-Daagh' 'Aaftab-e-Daagh' and 'Mahtab-e-
died in 1905.

दाग़ देहलवी

ख़ातिर से या लिहाज़ से मैं मान तो गया
झूठी क़सम से आपका ईमान तो गया

दिल लेके मुफ्त कहते हो कुछ काम का नहीं
उल्टी शिकायतें हुईं, एहसान तो गया

देखा है बुतक़दे में जो ऐ शेख कुछ न पूछ
ईमान की तो ये है कि ईमान तो गया।

होश-ओ-हवास-ओ-ताब-ओ-तवाँ 'दाग़' जा चुके
अब हम भी जाने वाले हैं सामान तो गया।

---

1. होश, सहनशक्ति।

Daagh Dehlvi

Out of consideration and concession, I trusted you
though
You have forfeited my trust by your insincere vow

She took away my heart free of cost
And rather than feel obliged, she blames the poor
heart

What I saw in the temple, O sheikh, ask me not
And say nothing of the faith, the faith is lost

I too am about to go, O Daag my luggage has
already been sent
Bearing and senses are gone, gone already
forebearance and strength

दाग़ देहलवी

उज्र आने में भी है और बुलाते भी नहीं
बाइस-ए-तर्क-ए-मुलाकात[1] बताते भी नहीं

खूब पर्दा है कि चिलमन[2] से लगे बैठे हैं
साफ छुपते भी नहीं, सामने आते भी नहीं

हो चुके क़त्अ ताल्लुक[3] तो जफ़ाएँ[4] क्यूँ हों
जिनको मतलब नहीं होता वो सताते भी नहीं

ज़ीस्त से तंग हो ऐ 'दाग' तो जीते क्यूँ हो
जान प्यारी भी नहीं, जान से जाते भी नहीं।

---

1. न मिलने का कारण, 2. पर्दा, 3. सम्बन्ध-विच्छेद, 4. अत्याचार।

Daagh Dehlvi

She invites not and also has objections to coming
And gives no reason for not meeting

What a veil! she sits by, a covering that more reveals than hide
She neither appears openly nor sits aside

Once you snap all ties, why expect fidelity
If you have nothing to do with him, why trouble somebody

Since you are fed up with life, O Daag, why not end it, so
You neither seem to love it nor would you let it go

Amir Meenai

(1829-1900)

Some writers are truly prolific. Amir Meenai is one of them. He is said to have written forty books, many of which remain unpublished. The manuscripts are now the valuable possession of Raza Library, Rampur. Amir Meenai who was also known as Amir Ahmed was born in 1829. His father died when he was only seven. He had his education in Lucknow where he studied Arabic, Sanskrit, and theology among other subjects. He was a disciple of the well known Lucknow poet Asar Lukhnavi. He was an established poet by 1853 when he was just twenty four. Although he was a mystic by training and temperament as also by family background, his poetry is pulsating with physical charm and gives us glimpses of ecstatic beauty. There is in his poetry a sharp awareness and engagement with physical world.

The best period of Minai's life was from 1859-1887 at Rampur. It was a period of fulfillment not only materially but also in the matter of literary reputation. Before this, he had worked as mufti (magistrate). He also went to Patna and Bhopal in search of patronage. A meeting with the Nizam of Hyderabad proved auspicious. The Nizam invited him to Hyderabad where he was well received by scholars and admirers. The Nizam especially liked his qasidas, the poems written in praise of the patron. In Hyderabad he stayed with Daagh Dehlvi. He kept indifferent health particularly after 1888 and died in 1900. He wrote poetry in its various forms but he is best known for his ghazals. Among his books are "Subh-e-Azal" and "Sham-e-Avadh".

अमीर मीनाई

नावक-ए-नाज़[1] से मुश्किल है बचाना दिल का
दर्द उठ-उठ के बताता है ठिकाना दिल का

हाए! वो पहली मुलाकात में मेरा रुकना
और उसका वो लगावट से बढ़ाना दिल का

जी लगे आपका ऐसा कि कभी जी न भरे
दिल लगाकर जो सुनें आप फ़साना दिल का

तीर पर तीर लगाकर वो कहा करते हैं
क्यूँ जी, तुम खेल समझते थे लगाना दिल का?

1. मानिनी का बाण।

Amir I.

It is indeed difficult to protect your heart against
that sharp shooter's art
The ache there is constantly pointing to the target
in the heart

How I rue my lingering on in our first meeting
And the encouragement she gave me through her
greeting

You will never like it to end, if you hear carefully
My heart's story

Shooting arrow after arrow, she would say
"Had you taken love for a child's play?"

Mohammad Iqbal

(1875-1938)

If one Indian, after Tagore, deserved a Nobel Prize for literature, it was Mohammad Iqbal. He, of course did not get it. He is among the greatest Indian poets. His poetry has the power to infuse life into a dying man. He advocates a life of struggle, a life of active virtue in order to realize our full potential. He is against all kinds of weakness, demoralisation, escapism and self-pity. His poetry sends out a clarion call to arise, awake or to be forever fallen, to use Milton's words. It is an exquisite poetry using powerful images, flowing like torrent and sweeping the reader along with it. He is a master craftsman.

Iqbal came of a Kashmiri Brahmin family which had converted to Islam only two generations back. He was born in 1875 in Sialkot (Pakistan). His father, Noor Mohammad was a poor artisan and a very religious man. Iqbal passed his M.A. in Philosophy and went abroad for higher studies. He wrote a dissertation on 'Development of Metaphysics in Persia' and got a Ph.D. degree from Germany. The dissertation was published by the Munich University. Iqbal also qualified as a Barrister from London. He taught Arabic in London before returning to India in 1908.

Iqbal is a great nationalist poet, who later turned to Islam in a big way. Poems like 'Himalya', Tarana-e-Hind' and 'Naya Shivala' are shining examples of nationalist poetry. He also wrote on Indian icons like Swami Ram Tirth, Nanak, Ram and others.

Iqbal's stay in Europe had affected him greatly. After his return to India, he began to concentrate on the problems of the Muslim world and became their spokesman and saviour. Poems like 'Shikwa' and 'Jawab-e-Shikwa' are good examples of it. He was against the British rule and their exploitation of India, but surprisingly, he accepted knighthood in 1923 and became Sir Mohammad Iqbal. As a spokesman of the Indian Muslims, he participated in two Round Table conferences. He was president of all India Muslim League (Punjab Branch). The idea of Pakistan is also said to have originated with Iqbal. In his later life, he suffered from chronic bad health and died in 1938. He is indeed a most inspiring poet. His works in Urdu, among others, are 'Bange-Dran', Bal-e-Jabril and Zarb-e-'Kalim'. He wrote a number of books in Persian also.

इक़बाल

गेसु-ए-ताबदार[1] को और भी ताबदार कर
होश-ओ ख़िरद[2] शिकार कर, क़ल्ब-ओ-नज़र[3] शिकार कर

तू है मुहीत-ए-बेकराँ[4], मैं हूँ ज़रा सी आबजू[5]
या मुझे हमकिनार[6] कर! या मुझे बेकिनार[7] कर

मैं हूँ सदफ़[8] तो तेरे हाथ मेरे गुहर की आबरू
मैं हूँ खज़फ़[9] तो तू मुझे गौहर-ए-आबदार कर

बाग़-ए-बिहिश्त से[10] मुझे हुक्म-ए-सफ़र दिया था क्यूँ?
कार-ए-जहाँ[11] दराज़ है, अब मिरा इंतिज़ार कर

रोज़-ए-हिसाब जब मिरा पेश हो दफ़्तर-ए-अमल
आप भी शर्मसार हो, मुझको भी शर्मसार कर

---

1. चमकीली लटें, 2. बुद्धि और चेतना, 3. हृदय और दृष्टि, 4. असीम, 5. नदी, 6. बगलगीर, 7. व्यापक, 8. सीपी, 9. ठीकरा, 10. स्वर्ग, 11. संसार का काम।

Iqbal

Let your shining hair still brighter shine
Enthrall my sense and reason, my eye and this heart of mine

Thou art an ocean limitless, and I a little stream only
Either absorb me, or make me boundless like thee

If I am a shell, it is upto you, whether or not I hold a pearl
If I am a pebble, make a pearl out of the pebble

Why did you turn me out of the Garden of Eden, in the first place
There is much work to do on earth still, so let you wait now, your grace!

On the Day of Judgement, when they present my balance sheet
Let you also feel ashamed as you make me feel the heat

इक़बाल

सितारों से आगे जहाँ और भी हैं
अभी इश्क़ के इम्तिहाँ और भी हैं

क़नाअत[1] न कर आलमे[2]-ए-रंग-ओ-बू पर
चमन और भी, आशियाँ और भी हैं

अगर खो गया इक नशेमन तो क्या ग़म
मक़ामात-ए-आह-ओ फ़ुग़ाँ[3] और भी हैं

तू शाहीं[4] है परवाज़[5] है काम तेरा
तिरे सामने आसमां और भी है

इसी रोज़-ओ-शब में उलझ कर न रह जा
कि तेरे ज़मान-ओ-मक़ाँ[6] और भी हैं

गए दिन कि तन्हा था मैं अंजुमन में
यहाँ अब मिरे राज़दाँ और भी हैं

---

1. सन्तोष, 2. संसार, 3. आर्तनाद, 4. बाज़, पक्षी, 5. उड़ान 6. देश-काल।

Iqbal

There are worlds beyond, the stars too
And many more trials in love still to go through

Do not stop at this world of fragrance and colour
There are abodes still more, many more gardens, dear

What if that one abode you no longer keep
There are other places for you to sigh and weep

You are an eagle, your job is higher, and higher to fly
There are before you to climb, still many a sky

Within the space of day and night do not remain confined
There are more spaces and times for you still to find

Gone are the days when I was alone in the assembly
I have now here, my confidants in plenty

इक़बाल

ज़माना देखेगा जब मेरे दिल से महशर[1] उठेगा गुफ़्तगू का
मेरी ख़ामोशी नहीं है, गोया मज़ार[2] है हर्फ़े-आरज़ू[3] का

जो मौजे-दरिया लगी यह कहने सफ़र से क़ायम है शान मेरी
गुहर[4] यह बोला सदफ़-नशीनी[5] है मुझको सामान आबरू का

कोई दिल ऐसा नज़र न आया, न जिसमें ख़्वाबीदा[6] हो तमन्ना
इलाही तेरा जहान क्या है, निगारख़ाना है आरज़ू का

अगर कोई शै नहीं है पिनहां तो क्यों सरापा तलाश हूँ मैं
निगह को नज़्ज़ारे की तमन्ना है, दिल को सौदा है जुस्तजू का

न हो तबीयत ही जिनकी क़ाबिल वो तरबियत में नहीं सँवरते
हुआ न सरसब्ज़ रहके पानी में अक्से-सरू-ए-किनारे-जू[7] का

1. प्रलय (कब्रों में से मुर्दे उठाने का दिन), 2. कब्र, 3. आकांक्षाओं, 4. मोती, 5. सीपी में रहना, 6. सोई हुई, 7. नदी के किनारे के सर्व (वृक्ष) की परछाईं।

Iqbal

The world would see when my heart speaks up
like a blast
My silence is not silence, it is a grave of desire
first and last

As the wave in the river averred "my glory lies
in travel eternal"
"In residing in the shell lies my dignity" said the
pearl

Not a heart, which is not a house of desire, have
I seen
What is this world O Lord, but a gallery of longings
sharp and keen!

The heart yearns for fulfillment, the eye is longing
for the sight,
What is it that I am looking for day and night!

If there is no aptitude, education will hardly
anything mean
The shadow of the tree on the river bank will never
become green.

तराना-ए-हिन्द

सारे जहाँ से अच्छा हिन्दोस्तां हमारा।
हम बुलबुलें हैं इसकी ये गुलिस्तां[1] हमारा॥

गुरबत[2] में हों अगर हम, रहता है दिल वतन में।
समझो वहीं हमें भी दिल हो जहाँ हमारा॥

परबत वो सबसे ऊँचा हमसाया आस्मां का।
वो संतरी हमारा, वो पासबां[3] हमारा॥

गोदी में खेलती हैं इसकी हज़ारों नदियाँ।
गुलशन[4] है जिनके दम से रश्के-जनां[5] हमारा॥

ऐ आबे-रौदे-गंगा[6]! वो दिन हैं याद तुझको।
उतरा तेरे किनारे जब कारवाँ हमारा॥

मज़हब नहीं सिखाता आपस में बैर रखना।
हिन्दी हैं हम, वतन है हिन्दोस्तां हमारा॥

Iqbal

The Anthem of Hindustan

Better than the whole world is this Hindustan of ours
We are its nightingales, we sing in its bowers;

Even when we go abroad, at home we remain in thought
For we are, where remains our heart.

Our sentinel it is, it is our protector
The mountain, higher than the high, the neighbour of the sky;

In its lap a thousand streams play with glee
And make our garden bloom, make us the heaven's envy

O you fast flowing waters of Ganga, do you remember the day
When our caravan landed on your bank for ever to stay?

Religion can never teach hatred, it must be understood,
We all belong to India, and are bound by a common motherhood

यूनान-ओ-मिस्र-ओ-रोमा सब मिट गए जहाँ से।
अब तक मगर है बाक़ी नामो-निशां हमारा॥

कुछ बात है कि हस्ती मिटती नहीं हमारी।
सदियों रहा है दुश्मन दौरे-ज़मां[7] हमारा॥

'इक़बाल'! कोई महरम[8] अपना नहीं जहाँ[9] में।
मालूम क्या किसी को दर्दे-निहां[10] हमारा॥

1. बाग़, 2. विदेश, 3. रक्षक (चौकीदार) 4. बाग, 5. स्वर्ग के लिए ईर्ष्या का कारण, 6. गंगा नदी, 7. संसार चक्र, 8. भेदी, 9. संसार, 10. आन्तरिक पीड़ा

While the glories of Rome and Greece and Egypt
are a thing of the past
Our name and achievements still in the world last;

There is something in us that keeps us alive
For all the hostility of the world, we still survive

Nobody in the world, Iqbal, can share our sorrow
None can understand our grief, none can our
heartache know

(Indebted to a translation by Khushwant Singh)

नया शिवालय

सच कह दूं ऐ बिरहमन! गर तू बुरा न माने।
तेरे सनमकदों के बुत हो गए पुराने॥

अपनों से बैर रखना तूने बुतों से सीखा।
जंगो-जदल[1] सिखाया वाइज़[2] को भी खुदा ने॥

तंग आके मैंने आखिर दैरो-हरम को[3] छोड़ा।
वाइज़ का वाज़ छोड़ा, छोड़े तेरे फ़साने[4]॥

पत्थर की मूरतों में समझा है तू खुदा है।
ख़ाके-वतन का मुझको हर ज़र्रा देवता है॥

आ गैरियत के पर्दे इक बार फिर उठा दें
बिछड़ों को फिर मिला दें, नक्शे दुई मिटा दें

सूनी पड़ी हुई है मुद्दत से दिल की बस्ती
आ इक नया शिवालय इस देश में बना दें

दुनिया के तीर्थों से ऊँचा हो अपना तीरथ
दामाने-आसमां से इसका कलश मिला दें

The New Temple

If you don't mind O Brahmin, you should be told
That the idols in your temple have all grown old

You have learnt from them nothing but hostility towards your own,
To the maulvi also, God has only the path of battle shown;

I turned away from the temple because I was fed up with it
And leaving the Kaba also, I thought, quite fit;

You think in these idols of stone resides the God of thine
Every speck of my motherland's dust to me is divine.

Let us once again this era of hostility end,
Reunite the separated ones, towards unity our energies bend;

For ages now, our heart is in a dreary state
Let us now a temple new in this country create

With its dome touching the sky
Let our pilgrim place be higher than the high;

हर सुबह उठके गायें मंतर वो मीठे-मीठे
सारे पुजारियों को मै प्रीत की पिला दें

शक्ति भी, शांति भी, भक्ति के गीत में हो
धरती के वासियों की मुक्ति प्रीत में हो

---

1. युद्ध, 2. इस्लामी उपदेशक, 3. मन्दिर तथा काबे की चारदीवारी को, 4. कहानियाँ।

Let us sing every morning mantras sweet,
Let every priest now on have love's surfeit

Our song of devotion now should give us strength
and peace
And in love alone should lie our final release.

साक़ी

नशा पिलाके गिराना तो सबको आता है।
मज़ा तो जब है कि गिरतों को थाम ले साक़ी॥

जो बादाकश थे पुराने वो उठते जाते हैं।
कहीं से आबे-बक़ा-ए-दवाम[1] ले साक़ी॥

कटी है रात तो हंगामा-गुस्तरी[2] में तेरी।
सहर[3] क़रीब है अल्ला का नाम ले साक़ी॥

---

1. अमृत, 2. बिछौने के हँगामें में, 3. सुबह।

Saqi

To intoxicate somebody and then to see him fall
is quite easy
But the beauty lies in giving support to a falling
man, O Saqi

The drinkers of the old school are passing away
already
Procure from somewhere some elixir now O Saqi

Your night has passed in the turmoil of the bed
verily
The dawn is approaching now, remember Allah,
O Saqi.

Majaz Lukhnavi

(1911-1955)

If somebody can be called John Keats of modern Urdu poetry, it is Majaz Lukhnavi. He was indeed a genius. Majaz, whose full name is Asrar-Ul-Haq Majaz Lukhnavi was born in 1911. His father, Siraj-Ul-Haq was the first graduate of his town when the family moved to Lucknow. Majaz was for some time a student of St. John College Agra, and he graduated from Aligarh Muslim University. It was at Aligarh that he started writing romantic poetry that made him an instant hit among the students there. His poems like 'Nazr-e-Aligarh' were adopted as the anthem of the student union. He soon started writing on themes of social relevance. He sang of national independence and was a great supporter of women's emancipation. He thought of national independence not only as a political necessity but also as an aesthetic need and a pre-requisite for realizing our full potential.

Majaz joined All India Radio Delhi and worked for its journal 'Aawaz'. But he soon quit this job and became active in the Progressive Writers Movement (P.W.A.) He started publishing the literary journal 'Naya Adab' from Lucknow in collaboration with Sardar Jafri and Sibte Hasan. For some time, Majaz also worked as an assistant librarian at the Harding Library in Delhi. He had turned alcoholic and had to be admitted in a hospital in Ranchi for de-addiction, but to no avail. He died in Lucknow in 1955.

In Majaz's poetry, we find a blend of modern attitude, classical diction and romantic temperament He gives a lyrical quality to revolutionary poetry and poetry on social themes. 'Aawara', 'Rail' and 'Ek Nojawajan Khatoon Se' are among his very famous nazms. He wrote some memorable ghazals too. 'Aahang' is Majaz's well known poetic collection.

मजाज़ लखनवी

आवारा

शहर की रात और मैं नाशादो-नाकारा[1] फिरूं
जगमगाती जागती सड़कों पे आवारा फिरूं
ग़ैर की बस्ती है, कब तक दर-ब-दर मारा फिरूं
ऐ गमे-दिल क्या करूँ, ऐ वहशते-दिल क्या करूँ!

झिलमिलाते कुमकुमों की[2] राह में ज़ंजीर सी
रात के हाथों में दिल की मोहनी तस्वीर सी
मेरे सीने पर मगर दहकी हुई शमशीर[3] सी
ऐ ग़मे-दिल क्या करूँ, ऐ वहशते-दिल क्या करूं!

ये रूपहली[4] छाँव, ये आकाश पर तारों का जाल
जैसे सूफ़ी का तसव्वुर[5], जैसे आशिक़ का ख्याल
आह लेकिन कौन जाने, कौन समझे जी का हाल
ऐ ग़मे-दिल क्या करूं, ऐ वहशते-दिल क्या करूँ!

फिर वो टूटा इक सितारा, फिर वो छूटी फुलझड़ी
जाने किसकी गोद में आई ये मोती की लड़ी
हूक़-सी सीने में उठी, चोट-सी दिल पर पड़ी
ऐ ग़मे-दिल क्या करूँ, ऐ वहशते-दिल क्या करूँ!

Majaz Lukhnavi

The Vagabond

This nightfall in the city, and I wander aimless
and sad
On the awake and glittering roads, my aimless
wandering, O
How long in the alien city from door to door I go!
What do I do, O sad heart, my mad heart!

There is a chain of glittering lights all the way
The night holds in its hand the lovely image of
the morning ahead
But on my heart, I have a sword burning red—
What do I do, O sad heart, my mad heart!

This silvery shade, this net of stars on the sky
Like the philosopher's imagination, like the lovers
flight
But ah, who will know, who will feel my heart's
plight!
What do I do, O sad heart, my mad heart!

A star falls again, again there is a dancing light,
God knows in whose lap this garland of pearls
will go—
But there is a cry welling up, and on my heart
I feel a blow—
What do I do, O sad heart, my mad heart!

रात हँस-हँस के ये कहती है कि मैखाने[6] में चल
फिर किसी शाहनाज़े-लाल-रूख के[7] काशाने में[8] चल
ये नहीं मुमकिन तो फिर ऐ दोस्त वीराने में चल
ऐ ग़मे-दिल क्या करूँ, ऐ वहशते-दिल क्या करूँ!

हर तरफ़ बिखरी हुई रंगीनियाँ, रा'नाइयां
हर क़दम पर इश्रतें[9] लेती हुई अँगड़ाइयाँ
बढ़ रही हैं गोद फैलाए हुए रुसवाइयाँ
ऐ ग़मे-दिल क्या करूँ, ऐ वहशते-दिल क्या करूँ!

रास्ते में रुक के दम ले लूँ, मिरी आदत नहीं
लौटकर वापस चला जाऊँ, मिरी फ़ितरत[10] नहीं
और कोई हमनवा[11] मिल जाए, ये किस्मत नहीं
ऐ ग़मे-दिल क्या करूँ, ऐ वहशते-दिल क्या करूँ!

मुन्तज़िर है एक तूफ़ाने-वला[12] मेरे लिए
अब भी जाने कितने दरवाज़े हैं वा मेरे लिए
पर मुसीबत है मिरा अहदे-वफ़ा[13] मेरे लिए
ऐ गमे-दिल क्या करूँ, ऐ वहशते-दिल क्या करूँ!

जी में आता है कि अब अहदे-वफ़ा भी तोड़ दूँ
उनको पा सकता हूँ मैं, ये आसरा भी तोड़ दूँ
हाँ मुनासिब है, ये ज़ंजीरे-हवा[14] भी तोड़ दूँ
ऐ ग़मे-दिल क्या करूँ, ऐ वहशते-दिल क्या करूँ!

इक महल की आड़ से निकला वो पीला माहताब[15]
जैसे मुल्ला का अमामा[16], जैसे बनिए की किताब
जैसे मुफ़लिस[17] की जवानी, जैसे बेवा का शबाब[18]
ऐ ग़मे-दिल क्या करूँ, ऐ वहशते-दिल क्या करूँ!

I am egged on by the smiling night to head for
the tavern,
To the house of a blooming beauty bend,
And if this is not possible, proceed to the wilder
ness, O friend—
What do I do, O sad heart, my mad heart!

On every side I see colour and gaiety,
On every side expanded beauty,
But I'm proceeding towards infamy only—
What do I do, O sad heart, my mad heart!

To stop by and rest is not my habit
It's alien to my nature to turn back and go
And I'm not lucky enough to meet some friend,
I know—
What do I do, O sad heart, my mad heart!

A battalion of calamities awaits me though
A thousand doors will still open for me, I know
But my vow of fidelity, is my foe—
What do I do, O sad heart, my mad heart!

I feel like breaking this vow of fidelity now
I shall give up all hope of attaining her
To break this useless bond is perhaps better—
What do I do, O sad heart, my mad heart!

The pale moon emerges from behind the palace
Like the turban of a mullah, like a trader's book
Like a poor man's youth, like a youthful widow's
withered look—
What do I do, O sad heart, my mad heart!

दिल में इक शो'ला भड़क उट्ठा है, आख़िर क्या करूँ
मेरा पैमाना छलक उट्ठा है, आखिर क्या करूँ
ज़ख़्म सीने में महक उट्ठा है, आखिर क्या करूँ
ऐ ग़मे-दिल क्या करूँ, ऐ वहशते-दिल क्या करूँ!

जी में आता है ये मुर्दा चाँद-तारे नोच लूँ
इस किनारे नोच लूँ और उस किनारे नोंच लूँ
एक-दो का ज़िक्र क्या, सारे के सारे नोच लूँ
ऐ ग़मे-दिल क्या करूँ, ऐ वहशते-दिल क्या करूँ!

मुफ़लिसी और ये मज़ाहिर[19] हैं नज़र के सामने
सैकड़ों सुलताने-जाबिर[20] हैं नज़र के सामने
सैकड़ों चंगेज़ों-नादिर हैं नज़र के सामने
ऐ ग़मे-दिल क्या करूँ, ऐ वहशते-दिल क्या करूँ!

लेके इक चंगेज़ के हाथों से ख़ंजर तोड़ दूँ
ताज पर उसके दमकता है जो पत्थर तोड़ दूँ
कोई तोड़े या न तोड़े मैं ही बढ़कर तोड़ दूँ
ऐ ग़मे-दिल क्या करूँ, ऐ वहशते-दिल क्या करूँ!

बढ़के इस इन्दर-सभा का साज़ो-सामां फूँक दूँ
इसका गुलशन फूँक दूँ, उसका शबिस्तां[21] फूँक दूँ
तख़्ते-सुल्तां[22] क्या, मैं सारा क़स्रे-सुल्तां[23] फूँक दूँ
ऐ ग़मे-दिल क्या करूँ, ऐ वहशते-दिल क्या करूँ!

---

1. उदास और बेकार। 2. बिजली की बत्तियों की, 3. तलवार, 4. चाँदी-रंग, 5. अनुध्यान, 6. मधुशाला, 7. लाल के फूल-ऐसे मुखड़े वाली के, 8. मकान में, 9. सुख-भोग, 10. स्वभाव या प्रकृति, 11. साथी, 12. विपत्तियों का तूफान, 13. प्रेम निभाने की प्रतिज्ञा, 14. वायु की ज़ंजीर, 15. चाँद, 16. पगड़ी, 17. निर्धन, 18. यौवन, 19 नज़ारे, 20. अत्याचारी बादशाह, 21. शयनागार, 22. बादशाह का सिंहासन, 23. शाही महल।

There is a fire in my heart, what should I do
My patience breaks apart, what shall I do
More I dress the wound, greater is the smart, what
should I do—
What do I do, O sad heart, my mad heart!

I feel like plucking out the moon and the stars
dead
Plucking out from this side, plucking out from that
Not one or two, but all of them, plucking out flat—
What do I do, O sad heart, my mad heart!

A state of penury here, and these sights before
my eyes
A Changez Khan and a Nadir Shah strutting
proudly
A thousand kings and their cruelty before me I
see
What do I do, O sad heart, my mad heart

I shall snatch the sword from Changez's hand and
break it apart
The glittering stone in his crown I must hit
Some body else may or may not, but I should break
It—
What do I do, O sad heart, my mad heart!

I should rise and burn all the paraphernalia in
Indra's court—
Burn this garden and set that bedroom ablaze
Why only the courtroom, the entire palace to the
ground raze—
What do I do, O sad heart, my mad heart!

नौजवान ख़ातून से

हिजाबे-फ़ित्ना-परवर[1] अब उठा लेती तो अच्छा था
खुद अपने हुस्न को पर्दा बना लेती तो अच्छा था

तिरी नीची नज़र खुद तेरी इस्मत की मुहाफिज़ है
तू इस नश्तर की तेज़ी आज़मा लेती तो अच्छा था

तिरी चीने-जबीं[2] खुद इक सज़ा कानूने-फ़ितरत में
इसी शमशीर से कारे-सज़ा[3] लेती तो अच्छा था

ये तेरा ज़र्द रुख़[4], ये खुश्क लब, ये वहम, ये वहशत
तू अपने सर से ये बादल हटा लेती तो अच्छा था

दिले-मजरूह को[5] मजरूहतर करने से क्या हासिल
तू आँसू पोंछकर अब मुस्करा लेती तो अच्छा था

अगर ख़लवत में[6] तूने सर उठाया भी तो क्या हासिल
भरी महफिल में आकर सर झुका लेती तो अच्छा था

तिरे माथे का टीका मर्द की क़िस्मत का तारा है
अगर तू साज़े-बेदारी[7] उठा लेती तो अच्छा था

सिनानें[8] खैंच ली हैं सर-फिरे बाग़ी जवानों ने
तू सामाने-जराहत[9] अब उठा लेती तो अच्छा था

तिरे माथे पे ये आंचल बहुत ही खूब है लेकिन
तू इस आंचल से इक परचम[10] बना लेती तो अच्छा था

(1937)

---

1. उपद्रवकर्ता पर्दा, 2. माथे का बल, 3. दंड देने का कार्य, 4. पीला मुखड़ा, 5. घायल हृदय को, 6. एकान्त में, 7. जागरण का साज़, 8. भाले, 9. शल्य-चिकित्सा-सम्बन्धी सामग्री, 10. पताका

Majaz Lukhnavi

To a Young Lady

Better, you had removed the malevolent veil now,
Better, you had put on a veil of your own beauty,

Your shyness is itself a guarantee of your dignity
You had better tested this weapon's efficacy

The crease on your forehead is a natural
chastisement—
You should have used this sword to award
punishment, instead.

Your pale face, your dry lips, your fears irrational—
Better, you had removed this cloud-cover from over
your head,

What use, further hurting the bruised heart,
You had better wipe your tears and smile prithee,

In private, if you raise your head, it is no use,
Even if you had to bow your head, you should
bow it before a full assembly.

The mark on your forehead is a star of man's future
You should be showing your awareness right

The young everywhere are rising in revolt
You should also be showing your might.

The veil sits lovely on your forehead though
You should have made it into a banner even so.

मजाज़ लखनवी

सारा आलम गोश-बर-आवाज़ है[1]
आज किन हाथों में दिल का साज़ है

हाँ ज़रा जुर्रत दिखा ऐ जज़्बे-दिल
हुस्न को पर्दे पे अपने नाज़ है

हमनशीं दिल की हक़ीक़त क्या कहूँ
सोज़ में डूबा हुआ इक साज़ है

आपकी मख़्मूर आँखों की क़सम
मेरी मय-ख़्वारी अभी तक राज़ है

छुप गए वो साज़े-हस्ती[2] छेड़ कर
अब तो बस आवाज़ ही आवाज़ है

हुस्न को नाहक़[3] पशेमाँ[4] कर दिया
ऐ जूनूं ये भी कोई अंदाज़ है

सारी महफ़िल जिसपे झूम उट्ठी 'मजाज़'
वो तो आवाज़े-शिकस्ते साज[5] है।

---

1. पूरा संसार आवाज़ पर कान लगाए है, 2. जीवन का संगीत, 3. बेवजह, 4. पश्चाताप, 5. टूटा हुआ साज़

Majaz Lukhnavi

The whole world is intently listening
Who is it today, holding my heart's string!

Show a little daring, O my heart's passion
So very proud of her veil is the beautiful one

Ask me not the condition of my heart, honey
It's a musical instrument drowned in agony

By your intoxicating eye, I swear
That my drinking is still a secret affair

She touched my life-string and hid away some-
where
Her voice only, now I hear

Unnecessarily I troubled the beautiful one—
O my passion, it is not done

On hearing which the whole mehfil O Majaz into
raptures went
It was the voice of a broken instrument

मजाज़ लखनवी

इज़्मे ख़िराम[1] लेते हुए आस्मां से हम
हटकर चले हैं रहगुज़रे-कारवां से[2] हम

क्योंकर हुआ है फाश[3] जमाने पे क्या कहें
वो राज़े-दिल जो कह न सके राज़दां से[4] हम

हमदम यही है रहगुज़रे-यारे-खुश-खिराम[5]
गुज़रे हैं लाख बार इसी कहकशां से[6] हम

क्या-क्या हुआ है हमसे जुनूं में न पूछिए
उलझे कभी ज़मीं से कभी आस्मां से हम

ठुकरा दिए हैं अक्लो-ख़िरद के[7] सनमकदे[8]
घबरा चुके थे कश्मकशे-इम्तिहां से हम

बख्शी हैं हमको इश्क़ ने वो जुर्रतें मजाज़
डरते नहीं सियासते-अहले-जहाँ से[9] हम

---

1. धीमी चाल से चलने का आदेश, 2. कारवान के रास्ते से, 3. प्रकट, 4. भेदी से, 5. सुन्दर चाल से चलने वाले यार (प्रेयसी) का मार्ग, 6. आकाशगंगा से, 7. बुद्धि और होश के, 8. मन्दिर, 9. संसार वालों की राजनीति से।

Majaz Lukhnavi

Instructed by heaven to go slow
On a road, away from the highway, we decided
to go

It became public knowledge, I know not how,
The secret, which even my confidant did not know

This is the road, O friend, which my beloved had
taken with her lovely gait
This is the milky way I travelled a million times
at any rate

What all we have gone through while in love, O
ask not
Sometimes, we had a tiff with the earth, some-
times, with heaven fought

Much harried by being put to test repeatedly
We have thrown common sense and discretion to
winds already.

On the strength of our love, O Majaz, we do and
dare,
About the politicking of the petty world, we do
not care

मजाज़ लखनवी

जुनूने-शौक़[1] अब भी कम नहीं है
मगर वो आज भी बरहम नहीं है

बहुत मुश्किल है दुनिया का संवरना
तिरी ज़ुल्फ़ों का पेचो-ख़म नहीं है

बहुत कुछ और भी है इस जहाँ में
ये दुनिया महज़ ग़म ही ग़म नहीं है

तकाज़े क्यों करूँ पैहम[2] न साक़ी
किसे यां फ़िक्रे-बेशो-कम[3] नहीं है

उधर मशकूक[4] है मेरी सदाक़त[5]
इधर भी बदगुमानी कम नहीं है

मेरी बरबादियों का हमनशीनो
तुम्हें क्या खुद मुझे भी ग़म नहीं है

अभी बज़्मे-तरब से[6] क्या उठूं मैं
अभी तो आँख भी पुरनम[7] नहीं है।

1. इश्क़ का उन्माद, 2. निरन्तर, 3. अधिक और कम की चिन्ता, 4. संदिग्ध, 5. सच्चाई, 6. खुशी की महफिल से, 7. सजल।

Majaz Lukhnavi

Intensity of my love is not less in any way
But she is not obliging even today

It is not your tangled hair, my dear—
It's very difficult to make this world better

It is not all sorrow and suffering only
The world has a lot else in its kitty

Why shouldn't I be demanding constantly
Who is not counting his loss and gain, here O
Saqi

Neither my perfect sincerity, she knows
Nor any the less her arrogance shows

For my ruin, O friend, in fact
Not only you, I too have no regret

How can I leave this world of gaiety yet
Even my eyes are not exactly wet

Josh Malihabadi

(1898-1982)

Shabbir Hasan Khan Josh Malihabadi, famously known as 'Shair-e-Inqalab' (the poet of revolution) was born in the year 1898. He came of a rich land–owning family of Afradi pathans. His father and grandfather were also poets. Josh got instruction in the art of poetry-writing from Waheedu Din Salim 'Panipati'. He was at Shanti Niketan for a short period in 1918. He went to Bombay and wrote for films too for a while. A famous editor of Urdu 'Aaj Kal,' a literary journal of the publication division of Govt. of India, Josh also edited "Kaleem" and "Naya Adab".

Josh was one of the persons close to Jawahar Lal Nehru. Nehru respected him for his poetry. So when in 1956, Josh decided to migrate to Pakistan, Nehru, it is said, was greatly hurt. And in Pakistan, as if as a punishment for this migration, he had a very bad time. He could never feel at home away from home; he could not adjust to the conditions there. It is said that when a group of friends from India, visited him in Pakistan, they found him reading Punjabi. "How come, Josh Sahib" one of them said, "the great Urdu, Arabic and Persian scholar is reading Punjabi?" "My friend" replied Josh, "I understand that the language of hell is Punjabi, and for my sin (of migration) I am sure I have to go to hell. So, I am reading Punjabi." His decision to go to Pakistan was indeed tragic.

Though he wrote some good ghazals, Josh is essentially a poet of the nazm. His range is very wide and one comes across variety of moods in his poetry. He is down to earth, romantic, moving, revolutionary, sensuous—all at the same time. He wrote many rubais too. He does not believe in writing of failed love; he is a poet of fulfillment. His is a very strident voice against oppression, cruelty, exploitation and tyranny. He is highly rhetorical and high-pitched rather than meditative or contemplative. He is a poet of the earth, His poems against the British rule in India like 'East India Company' and 'Bhagwati Revolt' became quite popular. However his language can sometimes be very difficult and off-putting. Apart from poetry, he wrote some ornate poetic prose. His autobiography "Yadon ki Barat" which he wrote in Pakistan became very famous. He wrote some criticism too. Among his other books are "Rooh-e-Adab", "Naqsh-e-Nigar" and "Harfo-Hikayat". Josh died in 1982 in Rawalpindi.

जोश मलीहाबादी

सोज़े-ग़म[1] दे के मुझे उसने ये इर्शाद किया[2]।
जा तुझे कश्मेकशे-दहर[3] से आज़ाद किया।

वो करें भी तो किन अलफाज़[4] में तेरा शिकवा।
जिनको तेरी निगहे-लुत्फ़[5] ने बर्बाद किया।

इतना मानूस[6] हूँ फितरत[7] से कली जब चटकी।
झुक के मैंने ये कहा, मुझसे कुछ इर्शाद किया?

मुझको तो होश नहीं, तुमको खबर हो शायद।
लोग कहते हैं कि तुमने मुझे बर्बाद किया।

---

1. ग़म की तपन, 2. फ़र्माया, 3. जीवन-संघर्ष, 4. शब्दों, 5. कृपादृष्टि, 6. परिचित, 7. प्रकृति।

Josh Malihabadi

She declares after making me addicted to sorrow :
You are relieved of suffering now, you may go

How can he complain against you, in what words
can he try
He, who has been ruined by your gracious eye

I am so familiar with the world of nature, that
just as a bud opened
"Did you say something to me?" I bowed my head
and enquired

I am in no position to say, but you may perhaps
know,
The rumour is that to you my ruin I owe

जोश मलीहाबादी

फ़िक्र[1] ही ठहरी तो दिल को फ़िक्रे-खूबां[2] क्यों न हो
ख़ाक होना है तो ख़ाके-कू-ए-जानाँ[3] क्यों न हो।

ज़ीस्त[4] है जब मुस्तकिल आवारागर्दी ही का नाम
अक़्लवालो! फिर तवाफ़े-कू-ए-जानाँ[5] क्यों न हो

इक न इक रिफ़अत के आगे सिज़दा लाज़िम है तो फिर
आदमी महबे-सजूदे-सिर-खूबा क्यूँ न हो।

इक-न-इक जुल्मतं[6] से जब वाबस्ता रहना है तो 'जोश'
ज़िन्दगी पर साया-ए-ज़ुल्फे-परेशाँ[7] क्यों न हो।

---

1. चिन्ता, 2. अच्छी वस्तुओं की चिन्ता, 3. प्रेयसी की गली की खाक, 4. जीवन, 5. प्रेयसी की गली का चक्कर काटना, 6. अँधेरे, 7. अस्त-व्यस्त केशों की छाया।

Josh Malihabadi

If worrying is our destiny, then why not worry
about some beauty
If we have to become dust, then why not dust in
our love's lane be

If life means wandering eternal, O wise men
Why not wander about the street of the beloved
then

If it is our fate to bow our head to a higher entity
Then why not bow it before some exquisite beauty

If we are fated O Josh to be in darkness of one
or the other kind
Then why being under the shade of the tangled tresses
should we mind

जोश मलीहाबादी

ग़ुंचे![1] तेरी ज़िन्दगी पे दिल हिलता है
बस एक तबस्सुम के[2] लिए खिलता है
ग़ुंचे ने कहा कि, "इस चमन में बाबा
ये एक तबस्सुम भी किसे मिलता है।"

---

1. कली, 2. मुस्कान के।

Josh Malihabadi

Your life is so moving that only for a while
You blossom, O bud, for just a smile
"In this garden, O dear," said the bud
"Not many are lucky to smile even for a while"

Hafeez Jallandhari

(1900-1982)

Hafeez Jallandhri is one of the prominent Urdu poets who became particularly famous in Pakistan. He is the author of Pakistan's national anthem and is held in that country in great esteem. His long poem 'Shah Nama Islam' is a landmark in the history of Islamic literature.

Hafeez was born in Jallandhar in 1900 and had his early education there. He had a literary bent of mind from the beginning and won recognition as a poet quite early. He, however dreaded formal schooling and was particularly poor in Mathematics. He would play truant and would be regularly thrashed. Ultimately as he says "He ran away from the school" Hafeez's early life was a life of great hardship. He did all kinds of jobs to keep his body and soul together. Five of his brothers had died prematurely.

Although Hafeez did approach some people to correct his verse, he was his own critic and teacher. His poems have a flow and delight which sweep the readers along. 'Abhi To Mein Jawan Hoon. (I am youthful still, still I am young) best illustrates this poetic flow. His poetry is highly musical and bears the stamp of the poet. His masterpiece, however, is "Shahnama Islam" in which he presents the grandeur and glory of Islam most effectively. Also nazms like 'Tooti Hui Kishti Ka Mallah' attest to his being a good poet.

However, Hafeez's career is not spotless. The poet who was later revered in Pakistan had acted as a lackey of the British, and written propaganda poetry for them for which he was made Khan Bahadur. And in Pakistan, he turned fundamentalist rather than remaining a great universal poet. His collections of poetry are titled 'Nagam-e-Zar', 'Soze-o-Saaz' and 'Talkhaba-e-Shireen'.

Hafeez died in 1982.

हफ़ीज़ जालन्धरी

अभी तो मैं जवान हूँ!

(1)

हवा भी खुशगवार[1] है गुलों पे भी निखार है,
तरन्नुमे-हज़ार[2] है बहार पुर-बहार है,
कहाँ चला है साकिया?
इधर तो लौट इधर तो आ,
अरे ये देखता है क्या,
उठा सुबू[3], सुबू उठा।
सुबू उठा, प्याला भर, प्याला भर के दे इधर,
चमन की सिम्त[4] कर नज़र समा[5] तो देख बेख़बर,
वो काली काली बदलियाँ,
उफ़क़ पे[6] हो गईं अयाँ[7],
वो इक हुजूमे-मैकशाँ[8],
है सू-ए-मैकदा रवाँ[9]
ये क्या गुमां है बदगुमाँ समझ न मुझको नातवाँ[10]
ख्याले-जुहद[11] अभी कहाँ?
अभी तो मैं जवान हूँ!

(2)

इबादतों का ज़िक्र है निजात की[12] भी फ़िक्र है,
जुनून[13] है सबाब[14] का ख्याल है अज़ाब[15] का,
मगर सुनो तो शैख जी!
अजीब शै हैं आप भी!
भला शबाबो-आशिक़ी[16]
अलग हुए भी हैं कभी?

Hafeez Jallandhari

I am youthful still, still I am young

(1)

Pleasant is the breeze and for flowers a bloom time.
The nightingale is at its song, the spring at its prime
Where do you go, O Saqi dear
Come hither, come here,
What for do you wait, why hesitate,
Pick up the cup, fill it up,
Fill it up and give it hither
Look at the garden, feel the weather;
Like a crowd of drinking men
Marching on towards the tavern,
The thickening clouds on the sky
The thick dark clouds catch the eye;
You're mistaken, you are wrong, I am not weak,
I am strong
I am youthful still, still I'm young

(2)

No question of prayers yet
No desire yet for redemption
But Sheikhji, you are a strange person
Thinking all the time of pious deeds,
Thinking of where our sin leads,
But have you ever given a thought

हसीन जलवारेज़ हों[17] अदाएँ फितना-खेज़[18] हों,
हवाएँ इत्रबेज़ हों[19] तो शौक़ क्यों न तेज़ हों,
निगार-हाए फ़ितनागर[20]
कोई इधर कोई उधर
उभारते हों ऐश पर,
तो क्या करे कोई बशर[21]
चलो जी किस्सा मुख्तसर तुम्हारा नुक्ता-ए-नज़र[22]
दुरुस्त है तो हो, मगर,
अभी तो मैं जवान हूँ!

(3)

ये गश्त[23] कोहसार की[24] ये सैर जू-ए-बार की[25],
ये बुलबुलों के चहचहे ये गुलरुखों के[26] कहकहे
किसी से मेल हो गया,
तो रंजो-फिक्र खो गया
कभी जो बख़्त[27] सो गया
ये हँस गया वो रो गया,
ये इश्क़ की कहानियाँ ये रस भरी जवानियाँ,
उधर से मेहरबानियाँ इधर से लनतरानियाँ[28]
ये आस्मान ये ज़मीं,
नज़्ज़ारा-हाए दिलनशीं[29]
इन्हें हयात-आफ़रीं[30]
भला मैं छोड़ दूँ यहीं।
है मौत इस क़दर क़रीं[31] मुझे न आएगा यकीं,
नहीं नहीं, अभी नहीं,
अभी तो मैं जवान हूँ।

(4)

न ग़म कुशदो-बस्त का[32] बुलंद का न पस्त का,
न बूद का[33] न हस्त का[34] न वादा-ए-अलस्त का[35]
उमीद और यास[36] गुम,
हवास गुम, क़यास[37] गुम,

Can youth and beauty stand apart?
If the beauties are on view
And their gestures murderous too,
If the fragrant breezes blow
Love is indeed bound to grow.
Lovely faces, simply murderous
Here, there and every where
Excite your passion through and through
What can poor mortals do?
But to cut the matter short
Even if right thou art,
I am youthful still, still I'm young.

(3)

This walk along the mountain path,
This walk along the river side
These cackles of the blooming faces
The nightingales showering graces
This chance meeting with someone
No tension left, sorrow, none
Somebody unlucky, somebody sad
Somebody here exceedingly glad—
These are but the tales of love.
Here we have a youthful fare
Grace here, boastings there;
On the earth and the sky
Lovely sights all around
All around, this lovely fare—
How can I leave it there!
I cannot believe, O just yet
That my death is approaching near
Nevar, never, indeed, never
For, I am youthful still, still I'm young.

नज़र से आस पास गुम
हमा[38] बजुज़[39] गिलासगुम,
न मैं में कुछ कमी रहे क़दह से[40] हमदमी रहे,
नशिस्त[41] ये ज़मीं रहे यही हमाहमी रहे,
वो राग छेड़ मुतरिबा[42]
तरब-फ़ज़ा[43], अलम-रुबा[44]
असर सदा-ए-साज़[45] का
जिगर में आग दे लगा,
हर एक लब पे[46] हो सदा न हाथ रोक साक़िया,
पिलाए जा पिलाए जा,
अभी तो मैं जवान हूँ!

---

1. रुचिकर, 2. बुलबुल का गीत, 3. शराब की मटकी, 4. ओर, 5. समय, 6. क्षितिज पर, 7. प्रकट, 8. मद्यपों का समूह, 9. मधुशाला की ओर जा रहा है। 10. दुर्बल, 11. तपस्या का विचार। 12. मुक्ति की, 13. उन्माद, 14. पुण्य, 15. पापों का दण्ड, 16. यौवन और प्रेम, 17. जलवे दिखा रहे हों, 18. फ़ितने खड़े करने वाली, 19. सुंगधियाँ बिखेर रही हों, 20. फ़ितने उठाने वालों (माशूक़ों) के मुखड़े, 21. प्राणी, 22. दृष्टिकोण (विचार), 23. सैर, 24. पहाड़ी स्थान की, 25. नदी के किनारे की, 26. फूलों जैसे चेहरे वालों के, 27. भाग्य, 28. डींगें, 29. मनोहर दृश्य, 30. जीवन-वर्धक, 31. निकट। 32. खोलने और बाँधने का, 33. अतीत का, 34. वर्तमान का, 35. आदिकाल का प्रण (कुरान में एक स्थल पर आता है कि जब खुदा इंसान को बना चुका तो उसने उससे पूछा कि क्या मैं तेरा खुदा हूँ? इंसान ने उत्तर दिया, हाँ तू मेरा खुदा है। उसी ओर संकेत है) 36. निराशा, 37. अनुमान (लगाने की शक्ति) 38. सभी कुछ, 39. सिबाय, 40. प्याले से, 41. महफिल, 42. गायिका, 43. आनन्दवर्धक, 44. शोक को मिटा देने वाला, 45. साज़ की आवाज का असर, 46. होठों पर।

(4)

No tension about meeting and separation,
No tension about rise and fall,
Neither of present, nor of past
Nor of promises made last;
Hope gone, despair gone
Gone all senses, thoughts all—
Everything, except the glass—
Everything around doth fall

Let there be no want of drink
Let the cup full overflow
Let the mehfil be in place
On and on, let it go.

O thou singer, play the tune
That gives joy, takes away pain—
No pain, and joy entire,
The tune that sets my being afire
Let everybody hum this tune
Stay not your hand, O Saqi dear
Give me more, pour me here.
I am youthful still, still I'm young.

हफ़ीज़ जालन्धरी

हम ही में थी न कोई बात याद न तुम को आ सके।
तुमने हमें भुला दिया, हम न तुम्हें भुला सके॥

तुम ही न सुन सके अगर, किस्सा-ए-ग़म[1] सुनेगा कौन?
किस की ज़बां खुलेगी फिर, हम न अगर सुना सके॥

होश में आ चुके थे हम, जोश में आ चुके थे हम।
बज़्म का रंग देखकर सिर न मगर उठा सके॥

शौक़े-विसाल[2] है यहाँ, लब पे सवाल है यहाँ।
किस की मजाल है यहाँ, हमसे नज़र मिला सके॥

अहले ज़बां[3] तो हैं बहुत, कोई नहीं है अहले-दिल।
कौन तेरी तरह 'हफ़ीज' दर्द के गीत गा सके॥

---

1. ग़म की कहानियाँ, 2. मिलने की उत्सुकता, 3. भाषा-विज्ञ।

Hafeez Jallandhari

There was nothing special in me, so you never
cared to remember
You forgot me clean, but I could never forget you
ever

If you too can't hear my tale of woe, who shall?
Who else will dare open his mouth, if I too can't
tell

I had understood it all, I was with passion
seething
But could not raise my eyes in view of the mood
of the gathering

I am fired by a desire to meet, I am eager to know
my fate
Who has the courage here to see me in the eyes
straight!

There are many here who have a way with words,
but few a feeling heart,
And who can sing like you, Hafeez who else has
the art!

Jigar Muradabadi

(1890-1960)

उनका जो काम है वो अहले-सियासत जानें
मेरा पैग़ाम मुहब्बत है जहाँ तक पहुँचे

"What the politicians do is their business,
My message is a message of love as far as it reaches."

One of the greatest lyricists of the twentieth century, and perhaps the most popular, Jigar Muradabadi was born in Banaras in 1890. His full name was Ali Sikandar Jigar Muradabadi. Jigar was a poet of delicate and sweet feelings of love; there is lilt in his poems which becomes all the more captivating because of his wonderful voice. Love is for him a burning passion, sublimated by self-surrender and sufferings; it is a powerful yearning born out of separation from his beloved. However, it is not so much the subject matter of his poetry which won him a pride of place among the ghazal writers in Urdu language, it is his mastery over the ghazal form, his tender handling of it and his ability to lift his audience, along with him as he recited those ghazals.

Jigar, along with Majaz, Faiz and Firaq played a very important role in reviving the ghazal as the principal form of Urdu poetry in the twentieth century. Twentieth century has been a century of complexity and confusion, industrialization and war, partition, uprooting, rehabilitation and uncertainty and a rising tide of commercialism and communal hatred. Contemporary reality is too tough and complex to be treated in a ghazal with its limitation of one couplet theme and its traditional preoccupation with love, beauty, idealism etc. The important contribution of poets like Jigar is that, inspite of all this, ghazal is even today the most popular form of Urdu poetry. Jigar, though primarily a love poet, wrote on social and political problems, as also on man's search for identity, his yearning for peace and desire for self-fulfillment.

Jigar came from a very ordinary family. He worked for some time as a travelling salesman, selling sun-glasses. He had some education in Urdu and Persian at Muradabad. He is said to have got his early poems corrected by Daagh Dehlvi, though it looks improbable because Daagh died when Jigar was still very young. However, Daagh's influence is prominently present in Jigars's poetry.

Jigar Muradabadi became a legend in his lifetime and influenced a large number of poets like Majaz Lukhnavi, Majrooh Sultanpuri and Jan Nisar Akhtar. His prominent works include "Daag-e-Jigar", "Shofa-e-Toor" and "Atish-e-Gul". Jigar died in 1960 at the age of 70.

जिगर मुरादाबादी

मोहब्बत में क्या-क्या मुक़ाम आ रहे हैं
कि मंज़िल पे हैं और चले जा रहे हैं।

ये कह-कहके हम दिल को बहला रहे हैं
वो अब चल चुके हैं, वो अब आ रहे हैं।

वो अज़-ख़ुद[1] ही नादिम हुए जा रहे हैं
ख़ुदा जाने क्या-क्या ख़्याल आ रहे हैं।

वो आलम है अब यारो-अग़ियार[2] कैसे
हमीं अपने दुश्मन हुए जा रहे हैं

मिज़ाजे-गिरामी[3] की हो ख़ैर या रब
कई दिन से अक्सर वो याद आ रहे हैं।

---

1. स्वयं, 2. मित्र और शत्रु, 3. उनके स्वास्थ्य।

Jigar Muradabadi

O what stages in love we are going through
Even after arriving at the destination we continue

I am beguiling my heart telling it repeatedly
She has started already, she has arrived actually

She is feeling ashamed already, I seem to find
O God, what thoughts are passing through my
mind

What a stage, what can a friend or foe do!
We are our own enemies too

For days now, I am remembering him a good deal
May gracious God look after his weal!

जिगर मुरादाबादी

दुनिया के सितम याद, न अपनी ही वफ़ा याद
अब मुझको नहीं कुछ भी मुहब्बत के सिवा याद

क्या लुत्फ़ कि मैं अपना पता आप बताऊँ
कीजे कोई भूली हुई खास अपनी अदा याद

क्या जानिए क्या हो गया, अरबाब-ए-जुनूँ को
जीने की अदा याद न मरने की अदा याद

मुद्दत हुई इक हादसः-ए-इश्क़ को लेकिन
अब तक है तिरे दिल के धड़कने की सदा याद।

Jigar Muradabadi

I remember neither the cruelties of the world nor
my own fidelity
Except my love, I remember nothing absolutely

What is the fun, if I were to give my own in-
troduction
Try to recall some gesture of yours, now forgotten

To the fraternity of lovers, God knows what's
happening
They know neither the art of living nor do they
know the art of dying

The tragedy in love took place a long age ago
But I hear the sound of your pounding heart even
now.

जिगर मुरादाबादी

इक लफ़्ज़-ए-मुहब्बत का अदना यह फ़साना है
सिमटे तो दिल-ए-आशिक़, फैले तो ज़माना है

क्या हुस्न ने समझा है, क्या इश्क़ ने जाना है
हम खाक़नशीनों[1] की ठोकर में जमाना है

यह इश्क़ नहीं आसाँ इतना ही समझ लीजे
इक आग का दरिया है और डूब के जाना है

हम इश्क़ के मारों का इतना ही फ़साना है
रोने को नहीं कोई, हँसने को ज़माना है

आँसू तो बहुत से हैं आँखों में 'जिगर' लेकिन
बिंध जाए सो मोती हैं, रह जाए सो दाना है।

1. विनम्र, दीन-हीन

Jigar Muradabadi

This word 'love' is nothing more, nothing less, it may be said
Than the lover's heart, when shrunk, and the whole universe when spread

Beauty knows it not, love may not have even heard
That we the lowly of the world can any time kick the world

This love is not easy, it must be clearly understood
It is a river of fire, and you drown in it, and then come good

There is none to lament our lot, but the world laughs at us
Our story, the story of the love-lorn may be summed up thus

Tears in the eyes, O Jigar, are numerous indeed
The one that finds a shell is pearl, every other is a bead.

जिगर मुरादाबादी

साक़ी की हर निगाह पे बल खा के पी गया
लहरों से खेलता हुआ लहरा के पी गया

ज़ाहिद[1] ! ये मेरी शोखी-ए-रिंदाना[2] देखना
रहमत को[3] बातों-बातों में बहला के पी गया

ऐ रहमते-तमाम[4] ! मेरी हर खता मुआफ़
मैं इन्तिहा-ए-शौक़ में[5] घबरा के पी गया

पीता बगैर इज़्न के कब थी मेरी मजाल
दर-परदा चश्मे यार की शह पा के पी गया

उस जाने-मैकदा की क़सम, बारहा जिगर
कुल आलमे बसीत पे मैं छा के पी गया।

---

1. उपदेशक, 2. मद्यपों की चंचलता, 3. खुदा को, 4. खुदा, 5. उत्कंठा की चरम सीमा में।

Jigar Muradabadi

Tossed over by Saqi's every single glance, I drank
Dancing along with the waves' dance, I drank

Zahid, you should have seen my drinking glory
I beguiled even divinity, and drank.

Pardon me for all my sins, O gracious God
Overwhelmed by desire, I drank O Lord!

Without her permission, I would never dare to drink,
Egged on by my love's furtive glance, I drank

I swear by her, the soul and life of the tavern, O Jigar!
I prevailed over the whole world's expanse and drank.

Firaq Gorakhpuri

(1896-1982)

According to Ahmed Faraz, Firaq Gorakhpuri was the last great poet that India has produced. Firaq, whose full name was Raghupati Sahai Firaq Gorakhpuri, became a legend in his lifetime. He earned great fame and some notoriety. If he was reviled for being eratic, egocentric and alcoholic, he was admired for his sparkling wit, most engaging conversation and very incisive comments on poetry and society. He was unconventional and provocative as also highly controversial. A great poet, he was critcised for faulty use of language and meter. He was a Hindi-baiter, but a great admirer of Tulsi, Kabir, Raskhan and Bihari. Though he wrote in other genres of poetry too, his forte is ghazal and rubai (quartrain). His is a highly original and individual voice in Urdu ghazal. His poetry is a poignant expression of a poet strong both in feeling and thought.

Firaq is distinguished from other poets for filling his ghazals with the sweet smell of Indian soil and culture. In his collection of rubais 'Roop', one comes across different aspects of Indian culture, mythology and folklore. He liberated the Urdu ghazal poetry from Persian stranglehold and transformed its tone and climate.

Firaq belonged to a well-to-do Kayastha family. He learnt Urdu, Persian and Sanskrit from his father who was a poet in his own right and a leading lawyer of Gorakhpur. After he graduated from Allahabad in 1917, he was nominated to the civil service, which he refused to join. Instead he plunged into freedom struggle as a

Congressman and became under secretary of the Indian National Congress. He was arrested in 1920 and was lodged with Moti Lal and Jawahar Lal Nehru in Agra and Lucknow jails. Firaq later became a lecturer in English, first in Kanpur and then joined Allahbad University from where he retired in 1959.

Firaq led a life of acute loneliness. His marriage was a fiasco. He soon separated from his wife. In a way, his was a tragic life. His son, ashamed of his father's perverse sexual habits, committed suicide. Loneliness is a running theme in Firaq poetry. He was himself quite conscious, in fact too conscious of his greatness as a poet. Says

> आने वाली नसलें तुम पर रश्क करेंगी, हमअसरो
> जब उनको यह पता चलेगा तुमने फ़िराक़ को देखा है

> (Future generations will feel envious of you O my contemporaries,
> When they come to know that you have seen Firaq).

फिराक़ गोरखपुरी

किसी का यूँ तो हुआ कौन उम्र-भर फिर भी।
ये हुस्नो-इश्क तो धोखा है सब, मगर फिर भी॥

हज़ार बार ज़माना इधर से गुज़रा है।
नई-नई सी है कुछ तेरी रहगुज़र फिर भी॥

खराब होके भी सोचा किए तेरे महजूर[1]
कि तेरी नज़र है तेरी नज़र फिर भी॥

कहूँ ये कैसे, इधर देख या न देख इधर।
कि दर्द दर्द है फिर भी नज़र नज़र फिर भी॥

शबे-फ़िराक़[2] से आगे है आज मेरी नज़र।
कि कट ही जाएगी ये शामे-बेसहर[3] फिर भी॥

झपक रही हैं ज़मानो-मकाँ की भी आँखें।
मगर है क़ाफ़िला आमादा-ए-सफर[4] फिर भी॥

अगर्चे बेखुदी-ए-इश्क को ज़माना हुआ।
'फिराक़' करती रही काम वो नज़र फिर भी॥

---

1. वियोग-ग्रस्त, 2. वियोग की रात, 3. ऐसी संध्या या रात जिसकी सुबह न हो, 4. सफर के लिए तत्पर।

Firaq Gorakhpuri

Nobody loves anybody else forever though
Love and beauty are all a deception, even so

The world has travelled this road a thousand times though
Your pathway remains new even so

Even though destroyed in love, your lovers have had a soothing thought
That it was your eye after all that their ruin brought

I dare not say, see here or don't see
For, pain is pain after all, and your eye is free

My gaze is set beyond the evening of separation today
This dawnless night too, I'm sure will pass any way

The eye of the universe is blinking though
The caravan is even then all set to go

Although it is ages now when I was in love's frenzy
Her eye, Firaq, all the time kept doing its work quietly.

फ़िराक़ गोरखपुरी

छलक के कम न हो ऐसी कोई शराब नहीं।
निगाहे-नर्गिसे-रअना[1] तेरा जवाब नहीं॥

ज़मीन जाग रही है कि इंकिलाब है कल।
वो रात है कोई ज़र्रा भी महे-ख्वाब[2] नहीं॥

जो तेरे दर्द से महरूम हैं यहाँ, उनको।
ग़मे-जहाँ भी सुना है कि दस्तयाब[3] नहीं॥

अभी कुछ और हो इंसान का लहू पानी।
अभी हयात के चेहरे पर आबो-ताब[4] नहीं॥

दिखा तो देती है बेहतर हयात[5] के सपने।
ख़राब होके भी ये ज़िन्दगी ख़राब नहीं।

---

1. रमणीय नर्गिस (एक पुष्प का नाम जिसकी प्रेयसी की आँख से उपमा दी जाती है) की नज़र, 2. निद्रामग्न, 3. उपलब्ध, 4. चमक-दमक, 9. जीवन।

Firaq Gorakhpuri

There is no wine that decreases not when it spills out
O you Nargis like lovely eye, you are matchless without double

Tomorrow is the day of revolution, the whole world is awake
On a night like this, nobody will even a wink take

Those who cannot feel your sorrow, it is said
Are to the sufferings of the world too virtually dead

Let some more blood of man like water flow
On the life's brow as yet there isn't sufficient glow

Some glimpses of bright future can still be had
Even when it is bad, life isn't too bad

फ़िराक़ गोरखपुरी

सितारों से उलझता जा रहा हूँ
शबे-फ़ुर्क़त बहुत घबरा रहा हूँ॥

तेरे ग़म को भी कुछ बहला रहा हूँ
जहाँ को भी समझता जा रहा हूँ॥

यक़ीं ये है हक़ीक़त खुल रही है।
गुमाँ ये हैं कि धोखे खा रहा हूँ॥

असर भी ले रहा हूँ तेरी चुप का।
तुझे क़ायल भी करता जा रहा हूँ॥

जो उलझी थी कभी आदम के हाथों।
वो गुत्थी आज तक सुलझा रहा हूँ॥

Firaq Gorakhpuri

I am getting tangled with the stars, unwittingly
This evening of separation, I am at my wits' end already

I am getting over the sorrow caused by you
And at the same time understanding the world too

I am sure I am getting to know the reality
As also I feel I am deceived actually

I am absorbing your silence too
As also I am impressing you

The mess that Adam had made
I am trying to clean up till date

फिराक़ गोरखपुरी

सुकूते-शाम[1] मिटाओ, बहुत अँधेरा है।
सुख़न[2] की शमअ जलाओ, बहुत अँधेरा है॥

चमक उठेंगी सियाहबख़्तियाँ[3] ज़माने की।
नवा-ए-दर्द[4] सुनाओ, बहुत अँधेरा है॥

दियारे-ग़म[5] में दिले-बेक़रार छूट गया।
संभल के ढूँढ़ने जाओ, बहुत अँधेरा है॥

ये रात वो है कि सूझे जहाँ न हाथ को हाथ।
ख़यालो दूर न जाओ, बहुत अँधेरा है॥

पसे-गुनाह[6] जो ठहरे थे चश्मे-आदम में[7]।
उन आँसुओं को बहाओ, बहुत अँधेरा है॥

ये ग़म की रात तो कटती नज़र नहीं आती।
इक और रात बनाओ, बहुत अँधेरा है॥

गुज़श्ता अहद की[8] यादों को फिर करो ताज़ा।
बुझे चिराग़ जलाओ, बहुत अँधेरा है॥

थी एक उचटती हुई नींद ज़िन्दगी उसकी।
'फ़िराक़' को न जगाओ, बहुत अँधेरा है॥

---

1. संध्या की चुप्पी, 2. बातचीत, 3. दुर्भाग्य, 4. दर्द का गीत, 5. ग़म की नगरी, 6. पाप के पश्चात्, 7. मनुष्य की आँख में। 8. बीते दिनों की।

Firaq Gorakhpuri

Let the silence of the evening break, for it's very dark
Let the light of conversation overtake, it's very dark

It will begin to glow, the ill-fated world stark
Sing some sad song, O it is very dark

In the city of sorrow, my restless heart is lost
Tread carefully here, for it is very dark

The left hand knows not the right, such is the night
O thoughts, don't go afar, for it is very dark

The tears that human eye held back after the Sin Original
Shed them now, for it is very dark

This night of sorrow seems to have no end
Make a new night, for it is very dark

O rekindle the memories of past ages
Kindle again the blown out lamps, for it is very dark

Firaq's life was but a fitful sleep
O wake him not, for it is very dark

फ़िराक़ गोरखपुरी

कुछ इशारे थे जिन्हें दुनिया समझ बैठे थे हम।
उस निगाहे-आशना को[1] क्या समझ बैठे थे हम॥

रफ्ता-रफ़्ता[2] ग़ैर अपनी ही नज़र में हो गए।
वाह री ग़फ़लत[3], तुझे अपना समझ बैठे थे हम॥

इन्क़िलाबे-पै-ब-पै हर गर्दिशो, हर दौर[4] में।
इस ज़मीनो-आस्माँ को क्या समझ बैठे थे हम॥

भूल बैठी वो निगाहे-नाज़[5] अहदे-दोस्ती[6]।
उसको भी अपनी तबीयत का समझ बैठे थे हम॥

एक दुनिया दर्द की तस्वीर निकली, इश्क़ को
कोहकन और क़ैस[7] का क़िस्सा समझ बैठे थे हम॥

हुस्न को इक हुस्न ही समझे नहीं और ऐ 'फ़िराक़'।
मेहरबाँ नामेहरबाँ क्या-क्या समझ बैठै थे हम॥

---

1. परिचित नज़र को, 2. शनैः-शनैः, 3. असावधानी, 4. हर काल और हर कालचक्र में एक-के-बाद-एक क्रान्ति होती है। 5. नाज़ों भरी नज़र (प्रेयसी), 6. मित्रता का प्रण। 7. फ़रहाद और मजनूं।

Firaq Gorakhpuri

What we had thought was the world, turned out
to be some hints only
O, what all we had taken that familiar eye for,
so wrongly!

Gradually, I became stranger for myself too,
O, what a lack of awareness, for my own I had
taken you!

Revolution on revolution-that has been story of
every age
O how wrong about the sky and the earth has
been our image

All the promise of friendship, the proud one has
forgotten clearly
And we had thought that she had the same nature
as have we!

Love has turned out to be a story of pain
We had taken it for the heroics of Qais and Farhad
in vain

We had taken the beauty to stand O Firaq, for
anything but beauty
We kept associating with it things like kindness
and cruelty

फ़िराक़ गोरखपुरी

शाम भी थी धुआँ धुआँ, हुस्न भी था उदास उदास
दिल को कई कहानियाँ याद सी आके रह गईं

तारों की आँख भी भर आई मेरी सदा-ए-दर्द पर
उनकी निगाहें भी तिरा नाम बता के रह गईं

कौन सुकून दे सका ग़मज़दगान-ए-इश्क़[1] को
भीगती रातें भी 'फ़िराक़' आग लगा के रह गईं

---

1. इश्क के मारों को।

Firaq Gorakhpuri

The evening too was dusky and darkling, and sad
and sombre the beautiful one
A thousand stories seemed to cross the mind on
this occasion

Even the stars were moved by my cry of pain
Their eyes too seemed to indicate just your name

Who could give solace to a heart in love's plight
O Firaq, even the rainy night would only a fire
light

फ़िराक़ गोरखपुरी

शामे-ग़म कुछ उस निगाहे-नाज़ की बातें करो।
बेखुदी बढ़ती चली है, राज़ की बातें करो॥

नक़हते - ज़ुल्फे - परेशाँ, दास्ताने - शामे - ग़म[1] ।
सुबह होने तक इसी अंदाज़ की बातें करो॥

ये सुकूते-यास[2], ये दिल की रगों का टूटना।
ख़ामशी में कुछ शिकस्ते-साज़ की[3] बातें करो॥

कुछ क़फ़स की[4] तीलियों से छन रहा है नूर[5] सा।
कुछ फ़ज़ाँ[6], कुछ हसरते-परवाज़ की[7] बातें करो॥

जिसकी फुरक़त ने[8] पलट दी इश्क़ की काया 'फ़िराक़'
आज उसी ईसा-नफ़स दमसाज़[9] की बातें करो॥

1. उलझे हुए सुगंधित केशों और शोक-भरी संध्या (रात) का वृतांत, 2. नैराश्य की चुप्पी, 3. साज़ के टूटने की, 4. पिंजरे, 5. प्रकाश, 6. आकाश, 7. उड़ने की अभिलाषा, 8. बिछोह ने, 9. पवित्र-हृदय मित्र।

Firaq Gorakhpuri

Speak of those imperious eyes, O thou, this sad evening
A state of trance is overtaking me, say now in secrecy some thing

Story of some sad evening and of fragrance from the tangled hair
Till the morn arrives, serve only some such fare

This silence of despair, this breaking of the heart
O talk only of some broken instrument to enact this part

Some light through the bars of the cage is beginning to trickle by
Speak now of the sky, and of the desire to fly

Because of separation from whom the very state of love stands transformed, O Firaq
Let us today only of that noble friend talk

फ़िराक़ गोरखपुरी

सर में सौदा[1] भी नहीं, दिल में तमन्ना भी नहीं।
लेकिन इस तर्के-मोहब्बत का[2] भरोसा भी नहीं॥

ये 'ी सच है कि मोहब्बत में नहीं मैं मजबूर।
ये भी सच है कि तेरा हुस्न कुछ ऐसा भी नहीं॥

मेहरबानी को मोहब्बत नहीं कहते, ऐ दोस्त।
आह, मुझसे तो तेरी रंजिशे-बेजा[3] भी नहीं॥

मुद्दतें गुज़रीं, तेरी याद भी आई न हमें।
और हम भूल गए हों तुझे, ऐसा भी नहीं।

मुँह से हम अपने बुरा तो नहीं कहते कि 'फ़िराक़'।
है तेरा दोस्त, मगर आदमी अच्छा भी नहीं॥

---

1. उन्माद, 2. प्रेम के त्याग का, 3. अनुचित मनोमालिन्य।

Firaq Gorakhpuri

There is no madness in the head though, no desire
either in the heart any more
But I'm not sure that her love I'll continue to abjure

It's true that I am no longer for your love dying
But it is equally true that your beauty is no
ordinary something

Kindness is not love, O friend dear
Alas, you no longer against me even an unfair
grudge bear!

For years now, I have not thought of you, though
But that I have forgotten you either, that is not so

That Firaq is a bad person, I will not so far go
But he is not good either, he is your friend though

Shakil Badauni

(1916-1970)

Shakil Badauni is better known as a film lyricist than a poet of high literary merit. He is essentially a poet of love, manifesting it in its various moods and aspects. In this sense, his poetry could be called conventional. Shakil came under the spell of Jigar Muradabadi, who was a rage those days. "My poetry", says Shakil "attained its prime under Jigar's influence". The two of them would go to a mushaira sometimes together and overshadow every other poet there.

Shakil was born in Badayoon (U.P.) in 1916. His father Jalil Ahmed Kadri was also a poet. So was his uncle Zia Kadri, under whose guidance Shakil started writing poetry. His early education took place in a religious atmosphere. Later he studied at Aligarh, after which he took up a job in the Civil Supplies department in Delhi. 'Ranaiyan' was his first volume of poetry, followed by 'Shabistan', 'Sanam-o-Harairi and 'Nagma-e-Firdos.' Impressed by his poetry, famous musician Naushad Ali called him to Bombay where a bright career awaited him.

Although Shakil did not concern himself much with politics or social problems, eminent progressive writers such as Sardar Jafri and Majrooh Sultanpuri praised his poetry. According to Sardar, Shakil's poetry has great sweetness and softness. Majrooh Sultanpuri says "Even though I am opposed to Shakil's philosophy and practice as a ghazal writer, I feel envious when I read a good couplet by him."

Shakil died in 1970 at a relatively young age of fifty-four.

शकील बदायूनी

ग़म-ए-आशिक़ी से कह दो रह-ए-आम तक न पहुँचे
मुझे खौफ़ है ये तोहमत मिरे नाम तक न पहुँचे

मैं नज़र से पी रहा था कि ये दिल ने बद्दुआ दी
तिरा हाथ ज़िन्दगी भर कभी जाम तक न पहुँचे

ये अदा-ए-बेनियाज़ी[1] तुझे बेवफा मुबारक
मगर ऐसी बेरुख़ी क्या कि सलाम तक न पहुँचे

जो निक़ाब-ए-रुख़ उठा दी तो ये क़ैद भी लगा दी
उठे हर निगाह लेकिन कोई बाम[2] तक न पहुँचे।

---

1. उपेक्षा-भाव, 2. छत।

Shakil Badauni

Let not the sorrow of love the common street hit
Lest, I am afraid, I should be blamed for it

I was drinking with mine eyes, when by my heart,
I was cursed
May your hand never reach the wine into which
you are immersed

Carry on with your indifference by all means, O
you the unfaithful one
But does it mean that you exchange not even a
formal salutation?

She agreed to lift the veil but had this condition
also laid.
Let every eye see, but none to the terrace be raised.

शकील बदायूंनी

आज वो भी इश्क़ के मारे नज़र आने लगे
उनकी भी नींद उड़ गई तारे नज़र आने लगे

किससे जाकर माँगते दर्द-ए-मुहब्बत की दवा
चारागर अब खुद ही बेचारे नज़र आने लगे

हम तो दरिया ही को समझे थे तलातुम-आफ़रीं[1]
आज तो साहिल प' भी धारे नज़र आने लगे

आँख वीराँ, दिल परीशाँ ज़ुल्फ बरहम लब ख़ामोश
यों तो वो कुछ और भी प्यारे नज़र आने लगे

दूर तक क्या चल सकेंगे राह-ए-उलफ़त में 'शकील'
जब अभी से तुम थके हारे नज़र आने लगे।

---

1. तूफ़ान उठाने वाला।

Shakil Badauni

Now even she seems to be love-lorn,
Losing her sleep, and by the passion torn

Who do we go to and ask for loveache's cure
The physician himself looks helpless unlike before

Only the river could be flooded, we had thought
Now even the banks are with inundation fraught

The heart in turmoil, the eye distraught, the lip
sealed and dishevelled hair—
For all this, she is looking lovelier than ever

How would you traverse the love's long road, O
Shakil
Already, sick and tired you seem to feel.

Faiz Ahmed Faiz

(1911-1985)

Twentieth century, especially after Iqbal's death in 1938, was dominated by progressive poets of whom Faiz Ahmed Faiz was the greatest. He is not just the poet of a particular school of thought; he is a complete poet, whose poetry elevates, delights and moves all lovers of poetry. Both in his poetry and life, he comes across as a low-key, soft-spoken, mild-mannered gentleman. This, inspite of the fact that he was a revolutionary poet. Romantic and modern traditions met in him, as also the classical mode and manner. He has the rare knack of imparting freshness and new meaning to old images, symbols and metaphors. This enables him to lodge his protest against the exploitative, oppressive and inhuman socio-economic reality, while at the same time retaining classical sweetness and softness in poetry.

As a famous critic, Mumtaz Hussain says, "In Faiz's poetry, if on the one hand we have the tradition of Majnu, on the other we have that of Mansoor."

Faiz was born in Sialkot (Pakistan) in 1911. He studied in Murray College Sialkot, Government College and Oriental College, Lahore. He was M.A. in English and Arabic. He was a college teacher, first in Amritsar and then in Lahore. In 1941, Faiz married an English woman, Alice George. He joined the army and rose to the rank of a Colonel. Faiz was implicated in the notorious Rawalpindi Conspiracy case for allegedly attempting to overthrow the Pakistan Government in 1951. He spent four years in jail. Most of his poems of 'Dast-e-Saba' and

'Zinda Nama' were written in jail. Faiz was in London for sometime and after his return, became principal of a college in Karachi. He worked also as the chief editor of 'Pakistan Times' and was in Beirut editing a journal in the midst of a shooting war.

Apart from Urdu, Faiz was a good Punjabi poet. He was a frequent vistior to India and was equally popular both in India and Pakistan, nay in the entire Urdu world. He died in 1985 in Lahore.

मुझसे पहली सी मोहब्बत मेरी महबूब न माँग!

मुझसे पहली सी मोहब्बत मेरी महबूब न माँग!
मैंने समझा था कि तू है तो दरख़्शां[1] है हयात[2]
तेरा ग़म है तो ग़मे-दह्र का[3] झगड़ा क्या है
तेरी सूरत से है आलम में[4] बहारों को सबात[5]
तेरी आँखों के सिवा दुनिया में रखा क्या है
तू जो मिल जाए तो तक़दीर निगूं हो जाए[6]
यूँ न था, मैंने फ़कत[7] चाहा था यूँ हो जाए
और भी दुःख हैं ज़माने में मोहब्बत के सिवा
राहतें[8] और भी हैं वस्ल की[9] राहत के सिवा
अनगिनत सदियों के तारीक बहीमाना तिलिस्म[10]
रेशमो-अतलसो-कमख़्वाब के बुनवाए हुए
जा-ब-जा बिकते हुए कूचा-ओ-बाज़ार में जिस्म
ख़ाक में लिथड़े हुए, खून में नहलाए हुए
जिस्म निकले हुए अमराज़ के[11] तन्नूरों से
पीप बहती हुई गलते हुए नासूरों से
लौट जाती है उधर को भी नज़र क्या कीजे
अब भी दिलकश है तेरा हुस्न, मगर क्या कीजे
और भी दुख हैं ज़माने में मोहब्बत के सिवा
राहतें और भी हैं वस्ल की राहत के सिवा
मुझसे पहली सी मोहब्बत मेरी महबूब न माँग।

---

1. प्रकाशमान, 2. जीवन, 3. सांसारिक चिन्ताओं का, 4. संसार में, 5. स्थायित्व, 6. सिर झुका ले, 7. केवल, 8. आनन्द, 9. मिलन की, 10. अन्धकारपूर्ण पाशविक जादू, 11. रोगों के।

Faiz Ahmed Faiz

Ask me not for love, O dear, like before

Ask me not for love, O dear, like before
With you around, I had thought, life is all aglow,
When I sorrow for you, I need not bother about
the sufferings of the world,
Your beauty gives permanence to the spring
season, I had thought
That nothing else is worthwhile in the world except
your eyes,
But that is not it;
There are other sorrows too in the world, apart
from the sorrows of love

And other joys besides the joys of union—
A web of brutal darkness woven over centuries,
Human bodies on sale in the street and the market
place,
Bodies bathed in dust and blood,
Diseased bodies with festering wounds—
The eye is arrested by all this, it cannot help;
Your beauty though is as attractive as before
There are other sorrows also in the world beside
the sorrows of love
And other joys apart from the joys of union.
Do not ask me, dear, for love like before.

मेरे हमदम मेरे दोस्त!

गर मुझे इसका यकीं हो, मेरे हमदम, मेरे दोस्त!
गर मुझे इसका यकीं हो कि तेरे दिल की थकन
तेरी आँखों की उदासी, तेरी सीने की जलन
मेरी दिल-जोई, मेरे प्यार से मिट जाएगी
गर मेरा हर्फ़े-तसल्ली[1] वो दवा हो जिस से
जी उठे फिर तेरा उजड़ा हुआ बेनूर दिमाग़
तेरी पेशानी से धुल जाएँ ये तज़लील के[2] दाग
तेरी बीमार जवानी को शिफ़ा[3] हो जाए
गर मुझे इसका यक़ीं हो, मेरे हमदम, मेरे दोस्त!
मैं तुझे भींच लूँ सीने से लगा लूँ तुझ को
रोज़ो-शब[4], शामो-सहर[5] मैं तुझे बहलाता रहूँ
मैं तुझे गीत सुनाता रहूँ हल्के, शीरीं
आबशारों के[6], बहारों के, चमन-ज़ारों के[7] गीत
आमदे-सुबह के[8], महताब के[9], सय्यारों के[10] गीत
तुझसे मैं हुस्नो-मोहब्बत की हिकायात[11] कहूँ
कैसे मग़रूर हसीनाओं के बर्फ़ाब से जिस्म
गर्म हाथों की हरारत में[12] पिघल जाते हैं
कैसे इक चेहरे के ठहरे हुए मानूस नुक़ूश[13]
देखते-देखते यकलख़्त[14] बदल जाते हैं
किस तरह आरिज़े-महबूब का[15] शफ़्फ़ाक बिलूर[16]
यक-ब-यक बादा-ए-अहमर से[17] दहक जाता है
कैसे गुलचीं के[18] लिए झुकती है खुद शाखे-गुलाब[19]
किस तरह रात का ऐवान[20] महक जाता है
यूँ ही गाता रहूँ, गाता रहूँ तेरी खातिर

Faiz Ahmed Faiz

If I were sure of it, my comrade, my friend

If I were sure of it, my comrade my friend
That the sadness in your eyes, the sickness of your heart
And discomfort in the chest
Can be cured by my affection, my love,
If I were sure that my comforting word
Is the anodyne that will clean up your desolate mind
And will bring back your lost pride,
And your sickly youth will bloom again,
If I were sure of it, my comrade my friend,
I would hug you to my heart,
And morning and evening, entertain you
With songs soft and sweet,
The songs of spring, the garden songs and the songs of waterfalls,
Songs of dawn, songs of moonlight and stars,
I would keep telling you tales of love and beauty :
How the cold and haughty beauties melt with the mere touch of a warm hand,
How the familiar furrows on a face suddenly disappear
How the glass-like cheeks of the beloved glow,
How on its own the rose-bough bends before the flower-picker

गीत बुनता रहूँ, बैठा रहूँ, तेरी खातिर
पर मेरे गीत तेरे दुःख का मदाबा[21] तो नहीं
नग़मा-ए-जर्राह[22] नहीं, मूनिसो-ग़मख़्वाह[23] सही
गीत नश्तर तो नहीं, मरहमे-ग़मख़्वाह[24] सही
तेरे आज़ार[25] का चारा नहीं नश्तर के सिवा
और ये सफ़्फ़ाक मसीहा[26] मेरे क़ब्ज़े में नहीं
इस जहाँ के किसी ज़ो-रूह के[27] कब्ज़े में नहीं
हाँ मगर तेरे सिवा, तेरे सिवा, तेरे सिवा!

---

1. ढारस का शब्द, 2. अपमान के, 3. स्वास्थ्य, 4. दिन-रात, 5. सुबह-शाम, 6. झरनों के, 7. बागों के, 8. सुबह के आगमन के, 9. चाँद के, 10. नक्षत्रों के, 11. कहानियाँ 12. गर्मी में, 13. परिचित नैन-नक्श, 14. एकाएक, 15. प्रेयसी के कपोलों का, 16. स्वच्छ कांच, 17. शराब की लाली से, 18. फूल चुनने वाले के, 19. गुलाब की शाखा, 20. महल, 21. इलाज, 22. शल्य चिकित्सक, 23. हमदर्द, 24. दुःख रूपी घाव का मरहम, 25. रोग, 26. निर्दयी चिकित्सक, 27. प्राणी के।

And how the night gets soaked in fragrance,
I would keep writing songs for you keep singing
for your sake;

But my songs are no cure for your sorrow;
They may give solace, but can perform no surgical
operation

And there is no cure of your ill except ruthless
surgery

And I am not such a surgeon,
In fact, nobody else in the world is
Except you, except you and you alone.

बोल...

बोल कि लब आज़ाद हैं तेरे
बोल, ज़बाँ अब तक तेरी है
तेरा सुतवाँ[1] जिस्म है तेरा
बोल कि जाँ अब तक तेरी है

देख कि आहनगर की[2] दुकां में
तुन्द[3] हैं शोले, सुर्ख़ है आहन[4]
खुलने लगे कुफ़्लों के[5] दहानें[6]
फैला हर ज़ंजीर का दामन

बोल, ये थोड़ा वक्त बहुत है
जिसमो-ज़बां की मौत से पहले
बोल कि सच ज़िंदा है अब तक
बोल कि जो कहना है कह ले

---

1. तना हुआ, 2. लोहार की, 3. तेज़, 4. लोहा, 5. तालों के, 6. मुँह।

Faiz Ahmed Faiz

Speak up

Speak up, for you are free to speak
Speak up, for as yet you are master of your tongue
Your sturdy body is as yet your own,
Speak up, for there is life in the body still.

See the flames leaping up
See the red iron hot
See the lock opening and chains loosening
At the blacksmith's shop.

Speak up, for the little time you have is a lot,
Speak up, let the whole truth come out,
Before the body dies and life ebbs away
Speak you up and say what you have to say.

फ़ैज़ अहमद फ़ैज़

कुत्ते

ये गलियों के आवारा बेकार कुत्ते
कि बख़्शा गया जिनको ज़ौक़े-गदाई[1]
ज़माने की फटकार सरमाया[2] इनका
जहाँ-भर की दुतकार इनकी कमाई
न आराम शब को न राहत सवेरे
ग़लाज़त में[3] घर, नालियों में बसेरे
जो बिगड़ें तो इक दूसरे से लड़ा दो
ज़रा एक रोटी का टुकड़ा दिखा दो
ये हर एक की ठोकरें खाने वाले
ये फ़ाक़ों से उकता के मर जाने वाले
ये मज़लूम मख़्लूक़[4] गर सर उठाए
तो इंसान सब सरकशी[5] भूल जाए
ये चाहें तो दुनिया को अपना बना लें
ये आक़ाओं की[6] हड्डियाँ तक चबा लें
कोई इनको एहसासे-ज़िल्लत[7] दिला दे
कोई इनकी सोई हुई दुम हिला दे

---

1. भीख माँगने की रुचि, 2. निधि, 3. गन्दगी में, 4. जनता, 5. घमण्ड, 6. मालिकों की, 7. अपमान की अनुभूति।

Faiz Ahmed Faiz

Dogs

'These stray dogs, loitering about in the streets
Living on beggary
Being stoned away by everybody
And rebuked by all and sundry—
They have no rest at night, no respite by day;
Tempt them with a loaf of bread
And make them fight each other if they became inconvenient
Kicked about by everybody
And ultimately starving to death,
This oppressed populacc, however, if it ever rises in revolt
They would show the haughty ones their place,
Eat up their tormentors alive
And make this world all their own—
If only somebody roused them shaking them by their tail,
If only somebody made them realize the disgrace in which they live!

फ़ैज़ अहमद फ़ैज़

निसार मैं तेरी गलियों पे....

निसार मैं तेरी गलियों पे ऐ वतन, कि जहाँ
चली है रस्म कि कोई न सर उठा के चले
जो कोई चाहने वाला तवाफ़ को[1] निकले
नज़र चुरा के चले, जिस्मो-जां बचा के चले
है अहले-दिल के लिये अब ये नज़्मे-बस्तो-कुशाद[2]
कि संगो-खिश्त[3] मुक़य्यद[4] हैं और सग[5] आज़ाद

बहुत हैं ज़ुल्म के दस्ते-बहाना-जू[6] के लिए
जो चन्द अहले-जुनूं तेरे नाम-लेवा हैं
बने हैं अहले-हवस[7] मुद्दई भी, मुन्सिफ़ भी
किसे वकील करें, किससे मुन्सिफ़ी चाहें
मगर गुज़ारने वालों के दिन गुज़रते हैं
तेरे फ़िराक़ में यूँ सुब्हो-शाम करते हैं

बुझा जो रौज़ने-जिंदां[8] तो दिल ये समझा है
कि तेरी माँग सितारों से भर गई होगी
चमक उठे हैं सलासिल[9] तो हमने जाना है
कि अब सहर[10] तेरे रुख़ पर[11] बिखर गई होगी
ग़रज़ तसव्वुरे-शामो-सहर मे[12] जीते हैं
गिरफ्ते-साया-ए-दीवारो-दर मे[13] जीते हैं

यूँही हमेशा उलझती रही है ज़ुल्म से ख़ल्क[14]
न उनकी रस्म नई है, न अपनी रीत नई
यूँही हमेशा खिलाए हैं हमने आग में फूल
न उनकी हार नई है न अपनी जीत नई

Faiz Ahmed Faiz

Let me bow before you

Let me bow before you, my country, where
It is ordained that none will walk the streets with
his head held high
And if some lover of yours must go around
He should go most cautiously with downcast eye
Where under the new rules of freedom and
discipline,
Dogs are at large while brick and stones are held
in thrall.

However, there are still enough of your lovers
around
To take on the tyrant there,
Though there is many a greedy one too
Who has become both a prosecutor and a judge;
And we know not whom to make our lawyer
And from where can we justice get—
Still we live on
And pass our days and nights remembering you.

Whenever through the prison window we look
outside in the dark
We surmise that the parting in your hair is filled
with stars
Whenever our fetters shine in the light, we
imagine

इसी सबब से फ़लक का गिला नहीं करते
तेरे फ़िराक़ में हम दिल बुरा नहीं करते

गर आज तुझसे जुदा हैं तो कल बहम[15] होंगे
ये रात भर की जुदाई तो कोई बात नहीं
गर आज औज पे[16] है तालए-रकीब[17] तो क्या
ये चार दिन की ख़ुदाई तो कोई बात नहीं

जो तुझसे अहदो-वफ़ा उस्तुवार[18] रखते हैं
इलाजे-गर्दिशे लैलो-निहार[19] रखते हैं।

---

1. परिक्रमा के लिए, 2. बंधन और मुक्ति की व्यवस्था, 3. ईंट-पत्थर, 4. कैद, 5. कुत्ते, 6. बहाना बनाने वाले के हाथ, 7. लोलुप, 8. कारागार का झरोखा, 9. बेड़ियाँ, 10. सुबह, 11. मुखड़े पर, 12. सुबह और शाम की कल्पना में, 13. दीवारों और दरवाज़ों के सायों की पकड़ में, 14. जनता, 15. इकट्ठे, 16. आकाश पर, 17. प्रतिद्वन्द्वी का भाग्य, 18. प्रेम निभाने की प्रतिज्ञा को सुदृढ़, 19. रात-दिन के क्रम का इलाज।

That your face is glowing in the morning sun—
That is, behind bars, though,
We live lost in thoughts of you.

Like this only, have the people fought tyranny
There is nothing new about it all—
Always like this, we have grown flowers in the fire
There is nothing new in their defeat and nothing
new about our victory, so

We don't mind our fate
Or feel sad that we are away from you
For, if we are separated today, we'll certainly meet tomorrow.
This separation of a mere night is a separation hardly
And if the enemy's star is on the ascendant today
It matters not,
For this temporary divinity is no divinity at all—
And those who are committed to love you
Know also how to tide over this lean phase too.

फ़ैज़ अहमद फ़ैज़

तन्हाई

फिर कोई आया दिले-ज़ार[1] ! नहीं, कोई नहीं
राहरौ[2] होगा, कहीं और चला जाएगा
ढल चुकी रात बिखरने लगा तारों का गुबार
लड़खड़ाने लगे एवानों में[3] ख़्वाबीदा[4] चिराग
सो गई रास्ता तक-तक के हर इक राहगुज़र[5]
अजनबी ख़ाक ने धुँधला दिए क़दमों के सुराग़[6]
गुल करो[7] शम्ए, बढ़ा दो मय-ओ-मीना-ओ-अयाग़[8]
अपने बेख़्वाब[9] किवाड़ों को मुक़फ्फल कर लो[10]
अब यहाँ कोई नहीं, कोई नहीं आएगा

---

1. दुःखी मन, 2. राही, 3. महलों में, 4. सोए हुए, 5. मार्ग, 6. चिह्न, 7. बुझा दो, 8. सुराही, प्याले और शराब उठा दो, 9. जिनकी आँखों में नींद नहीं, 10. ताले लगा लो।

Loneliness

Has somebody come, O sad heart? No, none at all,
It must be some passer-by, who will go his way;
The night is ending and the stars are dispersing apart,
The sleepy candles in the palaces sputter
And every pathway after a long wait has fallen asleep
The uncaring dust has obiliterated all foot-marks—
Blow out the candle, and remove the bottle and the chalice hence,
Close your sleepless eyes like a house locked
Nobody, nobody will come here now.

Jaan Nisar Akhtar

(1914-1976)

Perhaps no other poet had richer poetic atmosphere around him than Jaan Nisar Akhtar whose full name was Sayyad Jaan Nisar Hussain Rizvi. His father, uncle and grandmother were also poets and some of his other ancestors were well-known scholars. And his son Javed Akhtar is a very good poet and a leading lyricist writing for the films today. Jaan Nisar Akhtar was born in Gwalior in 1914. He had his early education in Gwalior and then went to Aligarh Muslim University. He was a lecturer in Urdu in Victoria College Gwalior and head of the department in Bhopal. His marriage with Safia further enriched his poetic environment. She was the sister of the famous Urdu poet Majaz Lukhnavi. Both Jaan Nisar and Safia became members of the Progressive Writers Movement (PWM). Jaan Nisar went to Bombay and wrote for the films for some time. In 1953 Safia died and he remarried. His life alternated between adversity and financial security and happiness. Finally his health deteriorated badly and he died of a heart attack in Bombay in 1976.

Jaan Nisar Akhtar wrote both ghazals and nazms and excelled in both. He wrote 'geet' and 'rubai' too. Whereas his ghazals have a tenderness of feeling and expression and a delicacy of tone, his nazms flow like torrent sweeping the reader along with them. He wrote seven books of poetry. Some of the well-known ones are 'Khak-e-Dil', 'Tar-e-Griban' and 'Nazar-e-Butan'. He won Nehru Award and Sahitya Akademi Award. His poetry has earthly warmth, charm of physical beauty and delicate expression. Jaan Nisar was indeed a very good poet.

आखिरी मुलाकात

मत रोको इन्हें पास आने दो
ये मुझसे मिलने आए हैं
मैं खुद न जिन्हें पहचान सकूँ
कुछ इतने धुँधले साए हैं

दो पाँव बने हरियाली पर
इक तितली बैठी डाली पर
कुछ जगमग जुगनू जंगल से
कुछ झूमते हाथी बादल से
यह एक कहानी नींद-भरी
इक तख़्त पे बैठी एक परी
कुछ गुन-गुन करते परवाने
दो नन्हे-नन्हे दस्ताने
कुछ उड़ते रंगीं गुब्बारे
बन्नो के दुपट्टे के तारे
यह चेहरा बन्नो बूढ़ी का
यह टुकड़ा माँ की चूड़ी का
ये मुझसे मिलने आए हैं
मैं खुद न जिन्हें पहचान सकूँ
कुछ इतने धुँधले साएँ हैं।

अलसाई हुई ऋत सावन की
कुछ सौंधी खुशबू आँगन की
इक टूटी रस्सी झूले की
इक चोट कसकती कूल्हे की

Jaan Nisar Akhtar

The Last Meeting

Stop them not, let them come,
They have come to meet me
They are such shadowy figures
That I may not even recognize them, though.

These feet on the greenery imprinted
A butterfly on the bough
Some swinging elephants from the clouds
Some fireflies twinkling from the forest
This drowsy, sleepy story
This fairy sitting on the throne
Some buzzing moths
A pair of small glove,
Some colorful balloons, flying
These sparkles on the bride's dupatta,
This old Banno's face
And a piece from the mother's bangle—
Stop them not, let them come
They have come to meet me;
They are such shadowy figures,
That I may not even recognize them, though.

The lazy, lazy, rainy season
Some sweet fragrance from the courtyard

सुलगी-सी अंगीठी जाड़ों में
इक चेहरा कितनी आड़ों में
कुछ चाँदनी रातें गर्मी की
इक लब पर बातें नर्मी की
कुछ रूप हँसी काशानों के
कुछ रंग हरे मैदानों के
कुछ हार महकती कलियों के
कुछ नाम वतन की गलियों के
मत रोको इन्हें पास आने दो
ये मुझसे मिलने आए हैं।
मैं खुद न जिन्हें पहचान सकूँ
कुछ इतने धुँधले साए हैं।

कुछ चाँद चमकते गालों के
कुछ भँवरे काले बालों के
कुछ नाज़ुक शिकनें आँचल की
कुछ नर्म लकीरें काजल की
इक खोई कड़ी अफसानों की
दो आँखें रोशनदानों की
इक सुर्ख़ दुलाई गोट लगी
क्या जाने कब की चोट लगी
इक छल्ला फीकी रंगत का
इक लॉकेट दिल की सूरत का
रूमाल कई रेशम से कढ़े
वो खत जो कभी मैंने न पढ़े
मत रोको इन्हें पास आने दो
ये मुझसे मिलने आए हैं
मैं खुद न जिन्हें पहचान सकूँ
कुछ ऐसे धुँधले साए हैं

कुछ उजड़ी माँगें शामों की
आवाज़ शकस्ता जामों की

A broken string from the wing
An aching injury of the hip
A warm hearth in winter
A face peeping through many a hole
Some moonlit summer nights
Some words from somebody's lips
Some lovely-looking houses
Some garland of fragrant flowers
Some names of the streets from my motherland—
Stop them not, let them come
They have all come to meet me;
They are such shadowy figures,
That I may not even recognise them, though.

Some cheeks shining like the moon
Some sable curls like the bumblebees
Some soft folds of the dress
Some delicate lines of the kajal
A forgotten part of the story
And ventilators opening like eyes
A red embroidered sheet
An image from the days long past
A ring with its lustre lost
A locket resembling the heart
A silk-embroidered handkerchief
Some letters that I never had read—
Stop them not, let them come
They have all come to meet me;
They are such shadowy figures,
That I may not even recognise them, though.

कुछ टुकड़े खाली बोतल के
कुछ घूँघरू टूटी पायल के
कुछ पुर्ज़े अपने दामन के
कुछ शे'र पुरानी ग़ज़लों के
उन्वान अधूरी नज़्मों के
टूटी हुई इक अश्क़ों की लड़ी
इक खुश्क कलम एक बंदघड़ी—
मत रोको इन्हें पास आने दो
ये मुझसे मिलने आए हैं
मैं खुद न जिन्हें पहचान सकूँ
कुछ ऐसे धुँधले साए हैं।

कुछ रिश्ते टूटे-टूटे-से
कुछ साथी छूटे-छूटे से
कुछ बिगड़ी-बिगड़ी तस्वीरें
कुछ धुँधली-धुँधली तहरीरें
कुछ आँसू छलके-छलके-से
कुछ मोती ढलके-ढलके से
कुछ नक्श ये हैरां-हैरां-से
कुछ अक्स ये लरज़ां-लरज़ां-से
कुछ उजड़ी-उजड़ी दुनियाएं
कुछ भटकी-भटकी आशाएँ
कुछ बिखरे-बिखरे सपने है
ये ग़ैर नहीं सब अपने हैं
मत रोको इन्हें पास आने दो
ये मुझसे मिलने आए हैं
मैं खुद न जिन्हें पहचान सकूँ
कुछ ऐसे धुँधले साए हैं।

Some widowed evenings
A sound of broken instruments
Some broken cups of wine
Some pieces of empty bottle
Some ghungroos from an anklet broken.
Some threads asunder from a female dress
Some parts of my own apparel
Some verses from a ghazal, old
And title of poems incomplete
A line of tears broken
A pen gone dry, a watch which had stopped
Stop them not, let them come
They have come to meet me;
They are such shadowy figures
That I may not even recognise them, though

Some relationships almost over
Some friends all forgotten
Some pictures badly drawn
Some write-ups dim and hazy
Some tears ready to burst
Some pearls fallen on the cheek
Some signs, all astonished
Some images, all afloat
Some world almost desolate
Some dreams nearly shattered—
They are all my own, they are no strangers;
Stop them not, let them come
They have come to meet me;
They are such shadowy figures
That I may not even recognise them, though

जाँ निसार अख़्तर

हर एक रूह में इक ग़म छिपा लगे है मुझे
ये ज़िन्दगी तो कोई बद-दुआ लगे है मुझे

मैं सो भी जाऊँ तो क्या? मेरी बन्द आँखों में
तमाम रात कोई झाँकता लगे है मुझे

मैं जब भी उसके ख़यालों में खो-सा जाता हूँ
वो खुद भी बात करे तो बुरा लगे है मुझे

दबाके आई है सीने में कौन-सी आहें
कुछ आज रंग तेरा साँवला लगे है मुझे

अब एकआध कदम का हिसाब क्या रखिए
अभी तक तो वही फासला लगे है मुझे

Jaan Nisar Akhtar

Some sorrow or the other is hidden in every heart
It seems that this life is a curse for the most part

I might fall asleep at night, but so what
Somebody seems to be peeping in my eyes, even when shut

Whenever I am lost in his thought
Even if he himself speaks, I like it not

What sighs are you hiding in your heart say you, pray
I find your complexion a little swarthy today

What if a step or two closer I get
The distance seems to be the same yet

Akhtar-ul-Iman

(1918-1996)

Akhtar-ul-Iman is by common consent a great modern poet, who has given a new direction to Urdu nazm both thematically and in the matter of style. He has widened the scope of the nazm bringing within its ambit themes like decline of civilization, oblivion and internal life, the struggle between good and evil and the conflict between dream and reality. In some of his poems, he deals with the tension between the inner and outer life. He attempts an understanding of outside reality as also of the complexity of individual's mental life. In order to fathom mysteries of creation, he sometimes uses interrogative style. Akhtar-ul-Iman was born in Najibabad in Bijnore District of U.P. After passing B.A., he worked in All India Radio, Delhi and the Civil Supplies Department. In 1945, he left for Bombay and took up dialogue writing in the films. Among his important works are 'Aabjoo', 'Yaaden', 'Beete Lamhe', and 'Naya Aahang'. He won Sahitya Academy Award for 'Yaaden' in 1962. He was a recepient of several other literary awards also.

Akhtar-ul-Iman was a great humanist. His concerns were profound. His poetry reflects his own sufferings as well as those of humanity in general. In the use of language, he was influenced by Miraji. It is a language different from the language of the ghazals; "It expresses a peculiar Indian sensibility." In most poems, he uses language of common conversation. Sometimes this language is quite coarse and looks unpoetic, but it heightens the poems' effect. A pathbreaking poet, Akhtar-ul-Iman has left a great legacy for Urdu nazm and has given it a new direction. Akhtar-ul-Iman died in 1996.

अख़्तर-उल-ईमान

एक सवाल

ज़मीन के तारीक गहरे सीने में फेंक
दो इसका जिस्म खाकी
ये सीम-गूँ नर्म-नर्म किरनें
जो माहो-अंजुम से फूटती हैं
ये नील-गूं आसमां की दुनिया
ये शर्को-ग़रब के किनारे
ये मेवा-हाए लज़ीज़ो-शीरीं
ये हुस्न-बेनाम के इशारे
कभी न इसको जगा सकेंगे
जवान दिलकश हसीन चेहरे से छीन ली
ग़म ने जो ताबानी
खुली हुई बदनसीब आँखें
ये देखती थीं कि आदमी ने
इक अपने ही जैसे आदमी पर
तमाभ दरवाज़े बन्द करके
वहशियत को जगा दिया है
और आखरिश ज़मीं की आग़ोश ने वफा की
इसीलिए क्या उगा करेंगे ये नर्म पौधे,
ये नर्म शाखें
कि इनको इक रोज़ हम उठाकर
खिज़ाँ की आग़ोश में सुला दें?

Akhtar-Ul-Iman

A Question

Throw his body in a ditch, deep and dark
The soft beams of the moon and the rays of the sun,
The blue sky and its huge expanse,
And this world from east to west,
These signals from some nameless beauty—
They will never be able to wake him up again.
Sufferings have killed all glow
On his face so lovely and youthful once;
The unfortunate wide-open eye, saw
How man has shut all doors
On a man like him;
All blessings of life
Lie covered in layers of darkness
And ultimately it is the mother earth
Which has taken him in her lap,
Will soft saplings, delicate branches
Again sprout and grow here
So that we can one day
Pluck and throw then
Into the bosom of the autumn once again!

उम्रे-गुरेज़ां के नाम

उम्र यूँ मुझसे गुरेज़ां है कि हर गाम पे मैं
इसके दामन से लिपटता हूँ, मनाता हूँ इसे
वास्ता देता हूँ महरूमी-ओ-नाकामी का
दास्ताँ आवला-पाई की सुनाता हूँ इसे
ख्वाब अधूरे हैं जो दोहराता हूँ उन ख्वाबों को
ज़ख्म पिन्हां हैं जो वो जख़्म दिखाता हूँ इसे
इससे कहता हूँ तमन्ना के लबो-लहजे में
ऐ मेरी जाँ, मेरी लैली-ए-ताबिन्दा-जबीं
सुनता हूँ तू है परी-पैकर-ओ-फरखंदा जमाल
सुनता हूँ तू है महो-महर से बढ़के हँसी
यूँ न हो मुझसे गुरेजां कि अभी तक मैंने
जानना तुझको कुजा, पास से देखा भी नहीं

सुबह उठ जाता हूँ जब मुर्ग अज़ाँ देता है
और रोटी के तआकुब में निकल जाता हूँ
शाम को ढोर पलटते हैं चरागाहों से जब
शब गुज़ारी के लिए मैं भी पलट आता हूँ

यूँ न हो मुझसे गुरेजाँ, मेरा सरमाया अभी
ख्वाब ही ख्वाब हैं, ख्वाबों के सिवा कुछ भी नहीं

मुलतवी करता रहा हूँ तेरी दीद को मैं
और करता रहा अपने लिए हमवार ज़मीं
आज लेता हूँ जो सोख़्ता रातों का हिसाब
जिनको छोड़ आया हूँ माज़ी के धुँधलके में कहीं

Akhtar-Ul-Iman

To the uncaring life

Life is turning its back on me at every step.
I try to clasp it, appeal to it, tell it my tale of failure and deprivation
Tell it of the blisters in my feet, of my unfulfilled dreams
And show it the wounds within;
I beseech it and say, O my love, you my life
I have heard that you are beautiful like a fairy,
Lovelier than the moon and the stars,
The smiling, the shining one
Do not turn your back on me, for as yet
Not to speak of knowing you, I have not even seen you well.

I rise early when the cock crows
And leave home in search of livelihood
And in the evening when the cattle return
I too come back home for the night's abode;
Do not turn your back on me, O life, for I have for my assets as yet
Only dreams and nothing else.
I have all the time been preparing for it.
And kept postponing my meeting with you
And now when I think of my days and nights of yore

सिर्फ नुकसान नज़र आता है इस सौदे में
कतरा-कतरा जो करे जमा तो दरिया बन जाए
ज़र्रा-ज़र्रा जो बहम करता तो सहरा होता
अपनी नादानी से अंजाम से गाफ़िल होकर
मैंने सालों को किया जमा, खसारा निकला
जानता तुझको कुजा, पास से देखा भी नहीं

यूँ न मुझसे गुरेजाँ हो, मेरा सरमाया अभी
ख्वाब ही ख्वाब हैं, ख्वाबों के सिवा कुछ भी नहीं

Lost in the hazy past
I reckon that I have only lost and lost;
If I had only collected you bit by bit
I would have had by now a fund vast
Far from knowing, I have even seen you not
O my love, my life, O thou shining one
Do not turn your back on me for as yet
I have only dreams and nothing else.

Sahir Ludhianvi

(1921-1989)

औरत ने जन्म दिया मर्दों को
मर्दों ने उसे बाज़ार दिया

(Woman gave birth to man, man made her
A commodity for the market.)

The poet who really and truly raised film songs to the level of high poetry, Sahir Ludhianvi was born in the year 1921 in Ludhiana (Punjab). His poetry is not only exquisite but has a strong social message also. Sahir was against all social institutions that tolerate exploitation and discrimination, encourage inequality and perpetrate cruelty. He was a friend of the poor and the oppressed although himself, he belonged to a rich landowning family. His father lived a luxurious life beyond his means. This was not liked by his mother and they were separated. Thus, Sahir had to undergo the trauma of living in a separated family. This left a permanent scar on his heart. This also explains his sympathy for the woman in the then (and even now) largely feudalistic society. Sahir was a rebel. After matriculation, he joined Government College, Ludhiana but was expelled from there for his participation in the activities of All India Students Federation, affiliated to the Communist Party of India, After that he joined Govt. College, Lahore from where also he was expelled for the same reason. In Lahore Sahir edited "Adab-e-Latif and "Savera". He then came to Delhi and from there moved to Bombay to settle permanently there.

Even when he was active in the students' movement, Sahir was seriously devoting himself to poetry, and he was soon established as a front rank Urdu poet. His poetry, not just his lyrics but also his nazms are soul-stirring. He was a progressive poet of great conviction and sincerity. Some of his verses like:

एक शहनशाह ने दौलत का सहारा लेकर
हम ग़रीबों की मुहब्बत का उड़ाया है मज़ाक

(An emperor on the strength of his power and pelf
has made fun of the poor lovers like us.)

have become classic. The only problem with Sahir, when one sits down with his collection, is monotony. Like Sahir, Faiz is also a progressive poet, but every poem has freshness about it. This is perhaps the reason why Sahir's poems are enjoyed only when they are read one or two at a time. This is also among the reasons that he is more popular than a great poet. However, his sincerity and his passion for a better future for the poor are remarkable.

Sahir's important poetic works are "Talkhiyan" (1944), "Parchchaiyan" (1955) and "Aau ke koi Khawab Dekhen" (1973). He is a recipient of Soviet Land Nehru Award and a Padamshree. Sahir died in 1980.

साहिर लुधियानवी

ताजमहल

ताज तेरे लिए इक मज़हरे-उल्फ़त[1] ही सही
तुमको इस वादी-ए-रंगीं[2] से अक़ीदत[3] ही सही

मेरी महबूब[4] कहीं और मिलाकर मुझसे—!

बज़्मे-शाही[5] में ग़रीबों का गुज़र, क्या मानी?
सब्त[6] जिस राह पे हों सतवते-शाही[7] के निशां
उस पे उल्फ़त भरी रूहों का[8] सफ़र क्या मानी?

मेरी महबूब पसे-पर्दा-ए-तश्हीरे-वफ़ा[9]
तूने सतवत[10] के निशानों को तो देखा होता
मुर्दा शाहों के मक़ाबिर से[11] बहलनेवाली!
अपने तारीक[12] मकानों को तो देखा होता

अनगिनत लोगों ने दुनिया में मोहब्बत की है
कौन कहता है कि सादिक़[13] न थे जज़्बे उनके
लेकिन उनके लिए तश्हीर[14] का सामान नहीं
क्योंकि वो लोग भी अपनी ही तरह मुफ़लिस[15] थे

ये इमारातो-मक़ाबिर[16] ये फ़सीलें, ये हिसार[17]
मुतलक़ुल्हुक्म[18] शहनशाहों की अज़मत[19] के सुतूं[20]
दामने-दहर[21] पे उस रंग की गुलकारी[22] है
जिसमें शामिल है तेरे और मेरे अज़दाद[23] का ख़ूँ[24]

Sahir Ludhianvi

Taj Mahal

The Taj may be a symbol of love for you,
You may be fascinated by its view
But meet me somewhere else my beloved, my dear

In the courts of kings, the poor have no place
A place where pelf and power rule, how can the loving souls find solace!

Behind this show of love you ought to have seen my dear
These signs of grandeur stark
You, who are beguiled by the dead kings' mausoleums
You ought to have remembered our houses dark

Numberless people have in this world loved
Who says their feelings were not true
But they could not advertise their lore
Because like us, they were poor too

These symbols of the aristocracy of kings and their imposing style,
The palaces and mausoleums, these ramparts and the forts here

मेरी महबूब! उन्हें भी तो मोहब्बत होगी
जिनकी सन्नाई ने[25] बख़्शी[26] है इसे शक्ले-जमील[27]
उनके प्यारों के मक़ाबिर रहे बेनामो-नमूद[28]
आज तक उन पे जलाई न किसी ने क़िन्दील[29]

ये चमनज़ार[30] ये जमना का किनारा, ये महल
ये मुनक़्क़श[31] दरो-दीवार, ये मेहराब, ये ताक़
इक शहनशाह ने दौलत का सहारा लेकर
हम ग़रीबों की मोहब्बत का, उड़ाया है मज़ाक

मेरी महबूब कहीं और मिलाकर मुझसे!

---

1. प्रेम का द्योतक, 2. रमणीय, 3. श्रद्धा, 4. प्रेयसी, 5. शाही दरबार में, 6. अंकित, 7. शाही वैभव के, 8. आत्माओं का (प्रेमियों का), 9. वफ़ा के विज्ञापन के पर्दे के पीछे, 10. वैभव, 11. मक़बरों से, 12. अंधकारपूर्ण, 13. सच्चे, 14. विज्ञापन, 15. निर्धन, 16. इमारतें और मकबरे, 17. क़िले, 18. स्वेच्छाचारी, 19. महानता, 20. स्तम्भ, 21. संसार के दामन पर, 22. बेल-बूटे, 23. पूर्वजों, 24. लहू, 25. कारीगरी ने, 26. प्रदान की, 27. सुन्दर रूप, 28. जिनका कोई नाम व निशान तक नहीं, 29. दीप, 30. उद्यान, 31. चित्रित।

This glow on the face of the earth
Is because of the blood of our ancestors, my dear

They too must have loved my dear
Whose art has given it a form so fair
But the graves of their beloveds have remained obscure
And nobody has lit a candle there

This garden here, this bank of river Yamuna, this mansion palatial,
These engraved walls and ceilings, doors and minarets with all the attendant fuss
An emperor on the strength of his wealth and riches
Has made fun of the poor lovers like us

Meet me somewhere else, my beloved dear

साहिर लुधियानवी

तंग आ चुके हैं कश्मकशे-जिन्दगी से हम
ठुकरा न दें जहाँ को कहीं बेदिली से हम

लो आज हमने तोड़ दिया रिश्तए-उमीद[1]
लो अब कभी गिला न करेंगे किसी से हम

उभरेंगे एक बार अभी दिल के वलवले
गो दब गए हैं बारे-ग़मे-ज़िन्दगी[2] से हम

गर ज़िन्दगी में मिल गए फिर इत्तफाक़ से
पूछेंगे अपना हाल तेरी बेबसी से हम

अल्लाह रे फ़रेबे-मशीयत[3] कि आज तक
दुनिया के जुल्म सहते रहे ख़ामुशी से हम

---

1. उम्मीद से सम्बन्ध, 2. जीवन की चिन्ताओं के बोझ से, 3. दैव इच्छा की प्रवंचना

Sahir Ludhianvi

The struggle and strains of life has driven me to the wall
I might kick the bucket in disgust, top bottom and all

From today, I'll expect nothing from any one
From today, I'll complain against none

My spirits will assert once again, I know
I am weighed down by the sorrows of life for now, though

If ever again we meet in life by any chance
I'll like to know my condition from your looks askance

What an irony, O god, what quirk of fate,
We're quietly suffering the cruelty of the world till this date

साहिर लुधियानवी

जब कभी उनकी तवज्जोह में कमी पाई गई
अज़-सरे-नौ दास्ताने-शौक़[1] दुहराई गई

बिक गए जब तेरे लब, फिर तुझको क्या शिकवा अगर
ज़िन्दगानी वादा-ओ-साग़र से बहलाई गई

कैसे-कैसे चश्मो-आ़रिज़[2] गर्दे-ग़म से बुझ गए
कैसे-कैसे पैकरों की[3] शाने-ज़ेबाई[4] गई

दिल की धड़कन में तवाज़ुन[5] आ चला है, ख़ैर हो
मेरी नज़रें बुझ गईं या तेरी रानाई[6] गई

उनका ग़म, उनका तसव्वुर[7] उनके शिकवे अब कहाँ?
अब तो ये बातें भी ऐ दिल! हो गई आई-गई

---

1. प्रेम-कथा, 2. आँखें और कपोल, 3. शरीरों की, 4. सज्जा, 5. संतुलन, 6. लावण्यता, 7. कल्पना।

Sahir Ludhianvi

Whenever I find her attention wandering
I retell the story of our love from the beginning

Once you have sold out your love why should you mind
If in the goblet and the bottle some solace I find

What beauties have been reduced to dust by the sorrows of time
What shapes and forms have lost their lustre and prime!

God save us, some normalcy in my heartbeat I see,
Am I going blind or, are you losing your charm and beauty?

Gone are my complaints against her, gone my suffering and my fancy high
These things too, O heart, are things of times gone by

साहिर लुधियानवी

चन्द कलियाँ नशात की[1] चुनकर
मुद्दतों मह्वे-यास रहता हूँ
तेरा मिलना ख़ुशी की बात सही
तुझसे मिलकर उदास रहता हूँ

1. हर्ष की।

Sahir Ludhianvi

I pick up some buds of happiness
And for long remain despair-clad
Meeting you is certainly a matter of joy
But after meeting you, I remain sad.

Kaifi Azmi

(1925-2003)

It was very late, often at 2 O'clock in the morning that Kaifi would recite his compositions at the mushiara (poetic symposium) after everybody else had recited. This was done not only in view of his seniority and stature as a poet, but also to hold the audience till the end. And when he recited his nazms and ghazals in his heavy, deep, sonorous voice, a voice, coming as if from the bottom of the sea, the audience would be more than rewarded. He was heard in pin-drop silence because of the seriousness and profundity of his thought and urgent relevance of his subject. He was not a prolific writer. But whatever he wrote bears the stamps of his considerable and peculiar poetic talent. He writes with a passion, has vigour, powerful expression and a breadth of vision. His writings reveal a modern sensibility and grasp of contempory situation.

Kaifi Azmi was born in Azampur, U.P. in 1925. He did not get opportunity for much formal education because in 1942, when he was just seventeen, he plunged into the Quit India Movement led by Gandhiji. Kaifi came from an orthodox religious family, but rebelled against all kinds of orthodoxy and against status quo. He joined Progressive Writers Movement and remained one of its leading members till the end. His missionary zeal, his passion and the force of his poetry owe much to his sympathy for the down-trodden and to his strident opposition to all forms of exploitation and oppression. He is a leading anti-imperialist poet. Some of his poems against Vietnam War are remarkable.

Kaifi Azmi published tour volumes of poetry, of which the most famous is 'Awara Sajde'. It is considered a valuable contribution to Urdu literature and has all the characteristics of Kaifi's poetry. Kaifi suffered from paralysis and died in 2003.

कैफ़ी आज़मी

सोमनाथ

बुतशिकन कोई कहीं से न आने पाए
हमने कुछ बुत अभी सीने में सजा रखे हैं
अपने सजदों में बसा रखे हैं।
दिल पे ये सोच के पथराव करो, दीवानो
कि जहाँ हमने सनम अपने छिपा रखे हैं,
वहीं ग़ज़नी के खुदा रखे हैं,
बुत जो टूटे तो किसी तरह बना लेंगे उन्हें
फिर से उजड़े हुए सीने में सजा लेंगे उन्हें
गर खुदा टूटेगा हम तो न बना पाएँगे
उसके बिखरे हुए टुकड़े न उठा पाएँगे
तुम उठा लो तो उठा लो शायद
तुम बना लो तो बना लो शायद
तुम बनाओ तो खुदा जाने बनाओ कैसा
अपने जैसा ही बनाया तो क़यामत होगी
प्यार होगा न ज़माने में मुहब्बत होगी
हमसे उसकी न इबादत होगी
वहशते बुतशिकनी देख के हैरां हूँ मैं
बुतपरस्ती मेरा शेवा है कि इंनसां हूँ मैं।

Kaifi Azmi

Somnath

No idol-breaker from anywhere should be allowed
to come here now;
Some idols we have set up right in our heart
And we bow before them religiously,
And if you must throw stones at our heart, O
the fanatic you
Remember that where our idols are situated
There Ghazni's god is seated too.
If you break them, we will somehow reassemble
the idols again
And place them in our desolate hearts
But if god is broken, at least we will not be able
to reassemble the parts
And build him again,
You may be able to
But if you were to build one, heaven knows, what
will that god be like!
But it will be a disaster if you make one in your
own image
For, there will neither be love in the world nor
affection then
And we will not be able to worship him.
I am amazed at the madness of the idol-breakers'
clan
For, idol-worship is my love, for, I am a man

एक लम्हा

जब भी चूम लेता हूँ इन हसीन आँखों को
सौ चराग़ अँधेरे में झिलमिलाने लगते हैं।
खुश्क-खुश्क होठों में जैसे दिल खिंच आता है
दिल में कितने आइने भरभराने लगते हैं
फूल क्या, शगूफ़े क्या, चाँद क्या, सितारे क्या
सब रक़ीब कदमों में सर झुकाने लगते हैं
ज़हन जाग उठता है, रूह जाग उठती है
नक्श आदमीयत के जगमगाने लगते हैं
घंटियाँ बजती हैं मंदिरों में रह-रहकर
देवता फ़िजाओं में मुस्कुराने लगते हैं
रक़्स करने लगती हैं मूरतें अजन्ता की
मुद्दतों के लब-बसता ग़ार गाने लगते हैं
फूल खिलने लगते हैं उजड़े-उजड़े गुलशन में
तश्ना--तश्ना गेती पर अब्र छाने लगते हैं
लम्हा भर को ये दुनिया, जुल्म छोड़ देती है
लम्हा भर को सब पत्थर मुस्कुराने लगते हैं।

Kaifi Azmi

A moment

When I kiss these lovely eyes
A hundred candles light up in the dark,
The dry lips pulsate with life
And many a mirror flash through the heart,
While the buds and the flowers, the moon and the stars—
All my rivals—before me bow.
The mind is stirred, the conscience awakes
And signs of nobleness begin to glow
The bells in the temple ring
And gods fill the atmosphere with smiles;
The sculptures of Ajanta begin to dance,
Silent caves come to life
And the dry land is covered with clouds,
And for a while the world gives up its cruel ways
For a moment, even the stones begin to smile—
When I kiss these lovely eyes.

कैफ़ी आज़मी

खारो-ख़स तो उठे, रास्ता तो चले
मैं अगर थक गया, काफ़ला तो चले

चाँद सूरज, बुजुर्गों के नक्शे-कदम
खैर बुझने दो इनको, हवा तो चले

इसको मज़हब कहो कि सियासत कहो
खुदकुशी का हुनर तुम सिखा तो चले

इतनी लाशें हैं, कैसे उठा पाऊँगा
आप ईंटों की हुरमत बचा तो चले

बेलचे लाओ, खोलो ज़मीं की तहें
मैं कहाँ दफ़न हूँ, कुछ पता तो चले।

Kaifi Azmi

Remove bramble and dry grass, let the road be cleared
At least the caravan should move, even if I am tired

Let the sun and the moon and the footprints of the ancestors into oblivion go
But the wind must blow

Call it your religion or politics, what you decide
You have taught us the way to commit suicide

You have enhanced though the prestige of the temple of brick and clay
How shall I be able to carry so many corpses away

Bring some shovels, dig up the earth below
And where I am buried, let me know

Ali Sardar Jafri

(1911-2002)

Sardar Jafri is a leading progressive poet of the twentieth century. All his life, he was associated with Progressive Writers Association, a body affiliated to the Communist Part of India. Sardar is fired with a mission which seeks to emancipate man from the stranglehold of exploitation and oppression, a mission that seeks equality and justice in society, and a mission that seeks to eradicate war and hostilities among nations. He is one of the greatest protagonists of Indo-Pak amity. His poetry has great power; it is passionate poetry, born out of great sincerity. Since he feels very strongly, his verses flow like a torrent. He is a consummate artist and has the knack of ending the poem where it moves the most and transports the reader to a higher plane of thought and feelings. His imagery particularly has a mark of individuality in which 'blood' occurs perhaps a little too often.

Sardar Jafri was born in 1911 in Balrampur in the state of Avadh. He joined Aligarh Muslim University but was soon rusticated from there for participating in the students' strike. He completed his BA from the old Delhi College, Delhi in 1938. In 1939, Sardar Jafri alongwith Majaz and Sibte Hasan started a literary journal, "Naya Adab". In 1940, he was arrested for taking part in an agitation against the British rule and was lodged in Banaras and Lucknow jails. Ultimately, he settled in Bombay and started working for the journal "Guftgoo". Sardar's works include "Khoon ki Lakir", "Nai Duniya ko Salam", "Asia Jaag Utha", Patthar ki Diwar", Ek

Khwab Aur" and "Lahu Pukarta Hai". Apart from these, he wrote a history of progressive literature, a book on Iqbal, "Iqbal Shanasi" articles on Meer, Kabir and Ghalib. Sardar Jafri has also edited "Divan-e-Ghalib" in Devnagri. He died in 2002.

सरदार जाफ़री

सुबहे-फ़रदा

(1)

इसी सरहद पे कल डूबा था सूरज होके दो टुकड़े
इसी सरहद पे कल ज़ख्मी हुई सुबहे-आज़ादी
ये सरहद खून की, अश्क़ों की, आहों की, शरारों की
जहाँ बोई थी नफ़रत और तलवारें उगाई थीं
यहाँ महबूब आँखों के सितारे तिलमिलाए थे
यहाँ माशूक चेहरे आँसुओं से झिलमिलाए थे
यहाँ बेटों से माँ, प्यारी बहन भाई से बिछड़ी थी
ये सरहद जो लहू पीती है और शोले उगलती है
हमारी ख़ाक के सीने पे नागिन बनके चलती है
सजाकर जंग के हथियार मैदां में निकलती है—
मैं इस सरहद पर कब से मुन्तज़िर हूँ सुबहे-फरदा का।

(2)

ये सरहद फूलों की, खुशबू की, रंगों की, बहारों की
धनक की तरह हँसती, नदियों की तरह बल खाती—
वतन के आरज़ों पर जुल्फ़ की तरह लहराती
पड़े इस पर न नज़रें खूँ के ताजर ताजदारों की
वो दिन आए कि आँसू बनके नफ़रत दिल से बहजाए
वो दिन आए कि ये सरहद बोसा-ए-लब बनके रह जाए

(3)

ये सरहद गुलशने-लाहौर की हवाओं की
ये सरहद अमनो-आज़ादी के दिल-अफ़रोज़ ख्वाबों की

Sardar Jafri

The New Dawn

The sun broke into two yesterday and set on this border,
Here only was the dawn of freedom wounded yesterday,
This border drawn with tears, blood and bullets,
Here stood the lovers casting wistful eye on each other,
Here they stood bathed in tears,
The mother from her sons and sister from brothers
Were separated here,
This border that drinks blood and spews fire
And like a serpent crawls on our chest,
This border that booms with guns and becomes a battlefield—
On this border, I have been waiting for a new dawn,
Waiting for a long while now.

(2)

This border should in fact be
A border of fragrance, colour, flowers and spring,
Smiling like a rainbow, running sportively like a stream
Swinging like a lovely curl on the nation cheek...

ये सरहद डूबते तारों, उभरते आफ़ताबों की–
ये सरहद मुरझाये कभी थे जो उन खिलते गुलाबों की
मैं इस सरहद पर कब से मुन्तज़िर हूँ सुबहे-फ़रदा का।

Would that it be safe from the evil eye
Of the rulers, trading in blood!....
Would that the day comes when hatred in the heart
Dissolves into tears
And the border becomes a kiss of love.

(3)

Would that this border becomes a perveyer of breezes from the gardens of Lahore,
It once again becomes a place where the dream of our freedom struggle was realized,
A place where in place of the twinkling stars, a full moon shines in full glory,
A place where withered flowers come into bloom one day
For a long time now, I have been waiting for that day.

सरदार जाफ़री

मेरा सफ़र

फिर इक़ दिन ऐसा आएगा।
आँखों के दिये बुझ जायेंगे
हाथों के कँवल कुम्लाएँगे
इक काले समुंदर की तह में
कलियों की तरह खिलती हुई
फूलों की तरह हँसती हुई
सारी शक्लें खो जाएँगी
ख़ूँ की गर्दिश दिल की धड़कन
सब रागनियाँ सो जाएँगी
और नीली फिज़ा की मखमल पर
हँसती हुई हीरे की कनी
ये मेरी जन्नत, मेरी ज़मीं
इसकी सुबहें, इसकी शामें
बेजाने हुए, बेसमझे हुए
इक मुश्त गुबारे-इन्सां पर
शबनम की तरह रो जाएँगी
हर चीज़ भुला दी जाएगी
यादों के हँसी बुतखाने से
हर चीज़ उठा दी जाएगी
फिर कोई नहीं ये पूछेगा
सरदार कहाँ है महफ़िल में।

लेकिन मैं यहाँ फिर आऊँगा
बच्चों के दहन से बोलूँगा
चिड़ियों की जुबाँ में गाऊँगा
जब बीज हँसेंगे धरती में

Sardar Jafri

My Journey

And then a day will come
When the eyes will switch off
And the lotus like hands, wither
And these faces, blooming all around me
Sink in a dark-dark sea,
The beauty of the heart and the tingling in the blood
Will cease to be
And this earth, this paradise of mine,
Shining like a diamond on the blue expanse
And all the mornings and the evenings
Will, on a speck of dust, called man
Knowing not why
Like the dew drops cry;
From the repertoire of memory
Everything will disappear
And there will be none to enquire
Where is Sardar gone!

But I will come back again,
And appear
In the form of the song of the sparrow and the children's lisp,
When the seeds sprout and the buds softly emerge from the earth

और कोपलें अपनी उँगली से
मिट्टी की तहों को छेड़ेंगी
मैं पत्ती-पत्ती, कली-कली
अपनी आँखें फिर खोलूँगा
सरसब्ज़ हथेली पर लेकर
शबनम के कतरे तोलूँगा
मैं रंगे-हिना, आहंगे-गज़ल
अंदाजे-सुखन बन जाऊँगा...
जाड़ों की हवाएँ दामन में
जब फसले-खिजाँ को लाएँगी।
रहरौ के जवाँ कदमों के तले
सूखे हुए पत्तों से मेरे
हँसने की सदाएँ आएँगी
धरती की सुनहरी सब नदियाँ
आकाश की नीली सब झीलें
हस्ती से मेरी भर जाएँगी
और सारा ज़माना देखेगा
हर किस्सा मेरा अफ़साना है
हर आशिक है सरदार यहाँ
हर महबूबा सुलताना है।

मैं एक तड़पता कतरा हूँ
मसरूफे-सफर जो रहता हूँ
माज़ी की सुराही के दिल से
मुस्तकबिल के प्याले में
मैं सोता और जागता हूँ
और जाग के फिर सो जाता हूँ
सदियों का पुराना खेल हूँ मैं
मैं मरके अमर हो जाता हूँ।

On every leaf, on every flower
I will appear,
And I will appear
On every dew drop,
I will be present in the colour of mehendi, in the ghazal's rhythm
And in the poet's song.

And when the winter winds
Herald the onset of autumn,
Through the dry leaves under the passer-by's feet,
I will laugh
All the golden streams on the earth
And all the blue lakes in the sky
Will, with my life be filled
And the whole world will see
That every story is my story
And every beloved, my beloved here.

I am a restless drop
Ever on the move
In the heart of the past, I sleep
And in the chalice of the future awake
And awake and sleep again.
I die and become immortal.
For centuries now this game has gone on.

Majrooh Sultanpuri

(1924-2000)

मैं अकेला ही चला था जानिबे-मंज़िल मगर
लोग साथ आते गये और कारवां बनता गया

(I had set out for the destination all alone. People came along and it became a caravan)

says Majrooh Sultanpuri, who was born in 1924 in Sultanpuri (U.P.) His full name is Asrar Hussain Khan Majrooh Sultanpuri. Majrooh had a traditional education in Urdu, Persian and Arabic at Sultanpur and later moved to Aligarh to continue his studies. He started his poetic career by writing geets and nazms, but after 1947 concentrated on the ghazal. He is one of those who have widened the frontiers of the ghazal to include in the genre revolutionary poetry and poetry of social concern, apart from the traditional romantic poetry. He has given a new dimension to the ghazal by enlarging the scope of the symbols used in it and by employing it to convey Marxist thought. He was a supporter of the progressive movement in literature and was actively associated with the Progressive Writers' Association, but he did not agree with some of the progressive writers that ghazal as a genre is inadquate for expressing social reality and revolutionary ideas.

Majrooh is best known as a writer of film songs. He had moved to Bombay from Aligarh and settled there. For his contribution to film industry, he was honoured with Dada Sahab Phalke Award. He won many other awards for his contribution in the field of ghazal. His poetic collection is also called 'Ghazal'. This collection has gone into very many editions with new pieces added to it from time to time. Majrooh died in 2000 in Bombay.

मजरूह सुल्तानपुरी

मुझे सहल हो गईं मंज़िलें वो हवा के रुख भी बदल गए
तिरा हाथ हाथ में आ गया सौ चिराग़ राह में जल गए

वो लजाए मेरे सवाल पर कि उठा सके न झुका के सर
उड़ी ज़ुल्फ चेहरे प' इस तरह कि शबों के राज़ मचल गए

वही बात जो वो न कह सके मिरे-शे'र-ओ-नग़मा में ढल गई
वही लब न मैं जिन्हें छू सका, क़दह-ए-शराब[1] में ढल गए

वही आस्तॉं[2] है, वही जबीं, वही अश्क़ है वही आस्तीं
दिल-ए-जार[3] तू भी बदल कहीं कि जहाँ के तौर बदल गए

मिरे काम आ गई आखिरश[4] यही काविशें, यही गर्दिशें
बढ़ीं इस कदर मिरी मंजिलें कि क़दम के खार निकल गए

---

1. शराब का प्याला, 2. चौखट, 3. दुखी दिल, 4. अंततः।

Majrooh Sultanpuri

Even the wind changed its course and the
destination became easy to reach
And a hundred candles were lit up as we held
our hand each to each,

She was so abashed at my question that she could
not raise her head right,
Even as the curl flew across her face, revealing
in full the essence of night

What she couldn't say was expressed in songs and
verses of mine,
The lips that I could not kiss, were kissed by the
cup of wine

The same threshold, the same forehead, the same
tears and the same sleeve to wipe them on!
You too should change, my heart, see how far the
world has gone.

Ultimately, my sufferings and my difficulties came
to my rescue
The journey being long, the thorns hurting my feet
came out too.

मजरूह सुल्तानपुरी

जब हुआ इरफ़ा तो ग़म आराम-ए-जाँ बनता गया
सोज़-ए-जानाँ दिल में सोज़-ए-दीगराँ बनता गया

मैं अकेला ही चला था जानिब-ए-मंज़िल मगर
लोग साथ आते गए और कारवाँ बनता गया

जिस तरफ भी चल पड़े हम आबला पायान-ए-शौक़
ख़ार से गुल और गुल से गुलस्तिाँ बनता गया

मैं तो तब जानूँ कि भर दे सागरे हर खासो-आम
यूँ तो जो आया वही पीरे-मुगाँ बनता गया

दहर में 'मजरूह' कोई जाविदाँ मजमूँ कहाँ
मैं जिसे छूता गया, वो जाविदाँ बनता गया।

Majrooh Sultanpuri

When understanding came, sufferings became a
source of solace
And others' sorrow took my own sorrow's place,

I had set out for the destination, at first all alone
Gradually, people came along, and it became a
caravan full-blown.

Whichever way we took, we who made light of
the blisters on our feet
The thorns became flowers, and the flowers turned
into a garden sweet

I will salute only him, who fills the cup for
everybody, big or small
Otherwise, everybody can pass off as master of
the tavern, tall

There is nothing immortal, O Majrooh, in the world
though
Whatever I touched with my pen, became so.

Nasir Qazmi

(1925-1975)

Nasir Qazmi is a leading Pakistani poet. Some of his ghazals are immensely popular. For instance, the ghazal beginning

दयारे-दिल की रात में चराग-सा जला गया
वो मिला नहीं तो क्या हुआ शक्ल तो दिखा गया

(He lit a candle in the night of my heart
He showed his face at least even if I met him not)

Nasir Qazmi, whose full name was Nasir Raza Qazmi was born in Ambala in 1925. He had his education in Ambala, Simla and Lahore. He belonged to a land-owning family and came back to Ambala in 1945 to look after his ancestral property. In 1947 after the partition of the country, he migrated to Lahore and became the chief editor of 'Humanyun'.

Nasir Qazmi is a poet in the tradition of Meer Taqi Meer. Like in Meer, there is note of melancholy and sadness in his poetry

वक्त अपना भी आयेगा 'नासिर'
ग़म न कर ज़िंदगी पड़ी है अभी

(Our time too will come, O Nasir
Don't lose heart, there is still a long life before us)

This mood of melancholy was accentuated by the murders and mayhem that the sub–continent witnessed after the partition of India. Families were separated, all plans for future and all dreams were shattered and survival became a big challenge. These human sufferings, lost love and struggle for survival find an echo in Nasir's poetry and, naturally, makes it sad and moving. Simplicity is a characteristic of his poetry.

Nasir Qazmi was associated with Radio Pakistan in Lahore. He was much influenced by the poetry of Akhtar Sheerani and wrote romantic poems and sonnets. He had started his poetic career in 1940 when he was just fifteen. Another influence on Nasir Qazmi, particularly in the field of ghazals, was that of Hafeez Hoshiarpuri. His collections of poetry are 'Narge-e-Ney', 'Deevan' and 'Sur ki Chhaya'. He died in 1975.

नासिर काज़मी

गए दिनों का सुराग़ लेकर किधर से आया किधर गया वो
अजीब मानूस अजनबी था, मुझे तो हैरान कर गया वो

बस एक मोती-सी छब दिखाकर, बस एक मीठी-सी धुन सुनाकर
सितारा-ए-शाम बनके आया, बरंगे ख्वाबे-सहर गया वो

खुशी की ऋतु हो या ग़म का मौसम, नज़र उसे ढूँढ़ती है हर दम
वो बुए-गुल था या नग़मा-ए-जाँ था, मेरे तो दिल में उतर गया वो

न अब वो यादों का चढ़ता दरिया, न फुर्सतों की उदास बरखा
यूँ ही ज़रा-सी कसक है दिल में, जो ज़ख्म गहरा था भर गया वो

वो रात का बेनवा मुसाफिर, वो तेरा शायर वो तेरा नासिर
तेरी गली तक तो हमने देखा था, फिर न जाने किधर गया वो

Nasir Qazmi

Carrying a clue to the days of yore, I know not
whence he came and where has he gone
It was a strangely familiar face that keeps me
wondering on

He just gave a glimpse pearl-like and played a
tune so sweet
He came like the evening star and is gone like
the morning dream

Be it the times of joy or the season of sorrow, my
eyes for him are always looking
The fragrance of a flower or a ravishing song,
whatever he was, he was my heart's king

There is neither the flood of memories now, nor
are there the long dull days of leisure
Only a little anguish remains in the heart, no longer
the deep wound that was there

That quiet nocturnal traveller, that poet of yours,
your Nasir
Coming upto your street, we saw him, God knows
where he has gone thereafter

नासिर काज़मी

दयारे-दिल की रात में चिराग़-सा जला गया
वो नहीं मिला तो क्या हुआ शक्ल तो दिखा गया

वो दोस्ती तो खैर अब नसीबे-दुश्मनाँ हुई
वो छोटी-छोटी रंजशों का लुत्फ़ भी चला गया

जुदाइयों के ज़ख़्म वो ज़िन्दगी ने भर दिए
तुझे भी नींद आ गई, मुझे भी सब्र आ गया

पुकारती है फुर्सतें कहाँ गईं मुहब्बतें
ज़मीं निगल गई उन्हें कि आसमान खा गया

गए दिनों की लाश पर पड़े रहोगे कब तलक
अलम-कशो उठो कि आफ़ताब सर पे आ गया

Nasir Qazmi

He lit a candle, so to say, in the night of my heart
He showed his face at least, even if I met him
not

Not to speak of that friendship of yore
Even the joy of feeling annoyed a little, is no more

Wounds of separation have been healed by the
life's pell-mell
I have learnt patience, and you too are sleeping
well

The hours of leisure demand to know where has
old love gone
Has the earth swallowed it up, or has the sky
preyed it on

How long will you cling to corpses of the days
gone by
Arise, you the afflicted people, for the sun is
already high on the sky

Hari Chand Akhtar

(1901-1958)

Hari Chand Akhtar, whose real name was Hari Chand Sharma, was born in Hoshiarpur (Punjab) in 1901. He was a disciple of Hafeez Jallandhari. He was M.A. in English as well as Persian, and wrote a number of articles and papers in Persian. He lived in Lahore upto 1947 and moved to Delhi after partition. In Delhi, he worked in the All India Radio, and since he was a disciple of Hafeez Jallandhari who was writing poems to lure the youth to enlist in army and fight on the side of the British, Hari Chand Akhtar too wrote in favour of participating in the second world war.

Hari Chand Akhtar wrote both ghazals and nazms as well as some good humorous poems which became quite famous. In the field of ghazal, he broke new ground. For his humorous poetry, he took the pseudonym Dozakhi (hellish). He was a very jocular person, and for once at least he was himself the subject of a good anecdote. Once a delegation from Pakistan was visiting India. Hari Chand complained that the Pakistani writers had forgotten their Indian counterparts. A member of the Pakistani delegation replied. 'No, we have given you at least a very important place in Pakistan; you are enshrined in our national flag, because "Hari means green, Chand means moon, and Akhtar means star, and all the 'three combine to make our national Flag". Those who have been with Hari Chand Akhtar, know him as a very witty and jovial person and remember some of his couplets. He died in 1958.

हरि चन्द अख़्तर

शबाब आया किसी बुत पर फ़िदा होने का वक्त आया
मिरी दुनिया में बन्दे के ख़ुदा होने का वक्त आया

उसे देखा तो जाहिद ने कहा ईमान की ये है
कि अब इन्सान को सजदा रवा[1] होने का वक्त आया

तकल्लुम[2] की खामोशी कह रही है हर्फ़-ए-मतलब से
कि अश्क़ आमेज़[3] नजरों के अदा होने का वक्त आया

हमें भी आ पड़ा है दोस्तों से काम कुछ यानी
हमारे दोस्तों के बेवफ़ा होने का वक़्त आया

नवेद-ए-सरबुलन्दी दी मुनज़्ज़िम[4] ने तो मैं समझा
सगान-ए-दहर[5] के आगे दुता होने का[6] वक़्त आया

---

1. नतमस्तक, 2. बातचीत, 3. आँसू भरी, 4. ज्योतिषी, 5. दुनिया के कुत्ते, 6. झुकना।

Hari Chand Akhtar

As I step into my youth, I feel like falling for
somebody
The time has come when humans, for me, will
assume divinity

As soon as he saw her, the zahid said, "honestly
speaking
Now the time has come for bowing and
beseeching."

The eloquence of his silence has only one meaning
That he is going to express himself through
weeping

I too need a favour now from my friends, which
means surely
The time has come for them to ignore me virtually

As the soothsayer said that I would rise high
I knew, I would have to cringe before the mean
and the sly

Makhmoor Dehlvi

(1909-1956)

मुहब्बत के लिए कुछ खास दिल मखसूस होते हैं
ये वो नग़मा है जो हर साज़ पर गाया नहीं जाता

(Only a few hearts are made for love. Love is a song which cannot be sung on every instrument.)

The writer of this famous couplet, Mukhmoor Dehlvi was born in Delhi in 1909. His real name was Fazal Ilahi who later came to be known as Dr. Fazal Ilahi. He was a disciple of Bekhud Dehlvi. He started writing poetry when he was only twelve years old. Makhmoor took up a job in Pataudi. Nawab of Pataudi was fond of poetry and Makhmoor became kind of a court poet of Pataudi (Haryana). He came back to Delhi in 1947 in the wake of communal unrest.

Makhmoor Dehlvi was basically a Mushaira (poetic symposium) poet where he was a hit. He was asked by the audience to recite more and more of his poems with the result that some of the other poets felt bad. He was the poet in the tradition of Daagh Dehlvi and had many illustrious disciples like Prem Lal Shifa. His first collection of poems 'Badaa-e-Makhmoor' appeared in 1952. This collection became quite popular. Makhmoor died in 1952. He had written

हमारे बाद अंधेरा रहेगा महफ़िल में
बहुत चराग़ जलाओगे रोशनी के लिए

(There will be gloom in the world of Urdu poetry, after me, however much you may try to light it up.)

There is a tradition of self-adulation in Urdu poetry and Makhmoor was not free from it.

'मख़मूर' देहलवी

किसी से मेरी मंज़िल का पता पाया नहीं जाता
जहाँ मैं हूँ फ़रिश्तों से वहाँ जाया नहीं जाता

मुहब्बत हो तो जाती है मुहब्बत की नहीं जाती
ये शोला खुद भड़क उठता है भड़काया नहीं जाता

फ़कीरी में भी मुझको माँगने से शर्म आती है
सवाली[1] हो के मुझसे हाथ फैलाया नहीं जाता

मुहब्बत के लिए कुछ ख़ास दिल मख़सूस[2] होते हैं
ये वो नग़मा है जो हर साज़ पर गाया नहीं जाता।

हर इक दाग़-ए-तमन्ना को कलेजे से लगाया है
कि घर आई हुई दौलत को ठुकराया नहीं जाता

---

1. याचक, 2. विशेष।

Makhmoor Dehlvi

Nobody can my destination know
Where I am, not even the angels can go

Love happens, it is not to be excited
It is a flame that doesn't have to be ignited

I find it hard to beg even in beggary
I just cannot stretch my hand and feel easy

Only a few hearts are for love especially made
It's a song which cannot be on every instrument
played

The scars of desires frustrated, I press to my heart
With the wealth unsought, it is not easy to part

Nushoor Wahidi

(1912-1983)

Nushoor Wahidi, whose real name was Hafeez-ul-Rehman was born in Balia district in U.P. in 1912. He had his early education in a spiritual atmosphere. Nushoor studied Arabic and Persian in Jaunpur and Urdu in Allahbad. Because of his family circumstances, he had to take up a teaching job at a very young age in 1926. Later, he settled in Kanpur and became a teacher of Arabic and Persian there. In 1947, he got a job in a college in Kanpur from where, he retired in 1972. In the meantime he had studied Unani medicine as well.

Nushoor Wahidi started writing poetry at the age of thirteen. At first, he wrote in Persian, but was advised to write in his mother tongue. Mohammad Rafi Sauda, Meer Taqi Meer and Faani Badauni were his favourite poets. Nushoor Wahidi was very popular at mushairas (poetic symposia) where he recited poetry alongside the great Jigar Muradabadi. It is a unique feature of Urdu poetry that some of its great poets like Iqbal, Firaq and Majaz have also been popular poets, liked both by the elite and the masses.

'Sahba-e-Hind', 'Shor-e-Nashoor' and 'Aatish-o-Nam' are Nashoor Wahidi's known poetic collection. Nashoor died in 1983, but to quote him

जो शहीदे-ज़ौके-हयात हो उसे क्यों कहो कि वो मर गया

(One who falls a martyr to life, why say he is dead.)

'नुशूर' वाहिदी

मैं अभी से किस तरह उनको बेवफ़ा कहूँ
मंज़िलों की बात है, रास्ते में क्या कहूँ

हुस्न-ए-बेहिजाब पर कोई पर्दा डाल लो
तुम उसे सनम कहो, मैं उसे खुदा कहूँ

गेसु-ए-सियाह की ये हसीं दराज़ियाँ
रात क्यूं कहूँ उन्हें, रात की दुआ कहूँ

तर्जुमान-ए-राज़ हूँ, यह भी काम है मिरा
उस लब-ए-ख़मोश ने मुझसे जो कहा, कहूँ

गैर मेरा हाल-ए-ग़म पूछते रहे मगर
दोस्तों की बात है, दुश्मनों से क्या कहूँ

इम्तिहान-ए-शौक़ है ऐसी आशिक़ी 'नुशूर'
दिल का कोई हाल हो, उनको दिलरुबा कहूँ।

Nushoor Wahidi

How can I label her unfaithful just yet
And about the destination, on the way, how can
I bet

Put a veil on her unveiled beauty
You may call her your beloved then, I will call
her a deity

With her tresses lovely, dark and long
Why call her the night, why not the night's prayer
song

I am an interpreter of secrets, this is also for me
to do
That I should interpret for you her silence too

The rivals kept enquiring why I was in so sad
a state
It is tale of friends, how can I to a foe relate

Love, O Nushoor is a wonderful test
Whatever the condition of my heart, I will call
her the best

Abdul Hamid Adam
(1909-1981)

Like many images, ideas, concepts and institutions such as Saqi, Raqeeb (rival) and Maikhana, the tradition of writing about wine-drinking in Urdu poetry has come from its Persian counterpart. This wine-drinking is not to be taken literally, it was a symbol of protest against the established order. Abdul Hamid Adam is a poet in this tradition. Bulk of his poetry is on wine drinking. He was born in Gujranwala (Pakistan) in 1901. His family had a tradition of service in the army. His father died when Adam was quite young. Adam worked as an officer in the Military Accounts Department. He also served in Iraq. For sometime, he lived in Rome also.

Like Sadat Hasan Manto and many others, Adam was a hard drinker

मैं मैकदे की राह से होकर निकल गया
वरना सफ़र हयात का काफ़ी तवील था

(Life's journey was extremely long.
I took a short cut through the tavern.)

Adam was a prolific writer who produced forty seven volumes of poetry. Some of his collections are 'Naqsh-e-davam', 'Dard-e-Mohabbat' and 'Dastan-e-Heer' a long poem. It is said, he would rattle up a poem in a few minutes, assemble a collection, sell it, and pay for his drinking. Apart from drinking, he wrote on love. According to Adam, poetry should be simple, spontaneous and crushing. He said "I don't just write poetry, I adore it." The fault with Adam as a poet, as with many others like Firaq and even Meer Taqi Meer is that they wrote too much and wrote indiscriminately. Their poetry needs rigorous editing. Adam died in 1981.

अब्दुल हमीद अदम

खाली है अभी जाम, मैं कुछ सोच रहा हूँ।
ऐ गर्दिशे-अय्याम[1], मैं कुछ सोच रहा हूँ॥

साक़ी तुझे इक थोड़ी-सी तकलीफ़ तो होगी।
साग़र को ज़रा थाम, मैं कुछ सोच रहा हूँ॥

इदराक[2] अभी पूरा तआवुन[3] नहीं करता।
दे बादा-ए-गुलफ़ाम[4], मैं कुछ सोच रहा हूँ॥

हल कुछ तो निकल आएगा हालात की ज़िद का।
ऐ कसरते-आलाम[5], मैं कुछ सोच रहा हूँ॥

---

1. समय के चक्कर, 2. बुद्धि, 3. सहयोग, 4. पुष्पवर्ण, मदिरा, 5. ग़मों के आधिक्य।

Abdul Hamid Adam

My cup is empty, yet, and I am lost in thought
I am lost in thought, O my indifferent lot

O Saqi, it will cause you a little inconvenience though
I am thinking something, hold the chalice for a while, so

My wits as yet are not fully cooperating
I am in a contemplative mood, give me a fragrant drink

There will be a way out of this dark alley too
O excess of sorrow, I am thinking of what to do

अब्दुल हमीद अदम

मयखाना-ए-हस्ती में[1] अक्सर हम अपना ठिकाना भूल गए।
या होश से जाना भूल गए या होश में आना भूल गए॥

असबाब तो बन ही जाते हैं तक़दीर की ज़िद को क्या कहिए।
इक जाम तो पहुँचा था हम तक हम जाम उठाना भूल गए॥

आए थे बिखेरे जुल्फों को इक रोज़ हमारे मरक़द[2] पर।
दो अश्क़ तो टपके आँखों से दो फूल चढ़ाना भूल गए॥

चाहा था कि उनकी आँखों से कुछ रंगे-बहाराँ[3] ले लीजे।
तरक़ीब[4] तो अच्छी थी लेकिन वो आँख मिलाना भूल गए॥

---

1. जीवन-रूपी मधुशाला में, 2. कब्र, 3. बहार का रंग, 4. अवसर, हेतु।

Abdul Hamid Adam

Often in the tavern, we forgot our place and zone
We forgot either to forget ourselves or come into
our own

Opportunities do come even when the times are
tough
The drink did reach us, though we failed to pick
it up

With her hair floating loose, to my grave she came
She did shed a tear or two, but offered no flowers
all the same

We wished to borrow from her eye some colours
of spring
The idea was good, but we could not look into
her eye, and it came to nothing

Qateel Shifai

(1919-2001)

Qateel Shifai is a popular Pakistani poet. His real name is Aurangzeb Khan. Qateel had his early education in Islamia Middle School, Rawalpindi. His studies were discontinued when his father died when Qateel was only nine years old. He took up a job, first as an octrio clerk and then as a transport manager in Murry. After that, he shifted to Lahore where he worked as the editor of 'Adab-e-Latif', a progressive literary journal.

Qateel Shifai is a progressive poet, but without any firm ideological commitment. Essentially, he is a romantic poet and his poetry reflects the healthy romantic spirit of Punjab exemplified, for instance, by the Heer-Ranjha Legend'. His romanticism is robust and intense and not the sickly kind, wallowing in self-pity. Besides his romantic poems, Qateel is at his best when he writes about women and presents some aspects of their life. In fact, he once jokingly said that people were jealous of him because he was popular among women. Most of his poems are light lyrical pieces which read like geets (songs). 'Hariyali' was the first collection of his songs . Though pleasing and popular, his poetry lacks profundity and depth. He is called a poet of the youth. And his range is also limited. He has written lyrics for films too. In certain respects, he is like Sahir Ludhianvi and Majaz Lukhnavi, though he lacks the intensity and burning passion of the latter. He published nine collections of poetry. Besides 'Hariyali', 'Gajar' 'Jhomar', 'Jal Tarang', 'Guftgoo' and 'Aawazon Ke Saye' are well known. Qateel died in 2001 at the age of eighty two.

क़तील शिफ़ाई

ये मोजिज़ा[1] भी मुहब्बत कभी दिखाए मुझे
कि संग[2] तुझ पर गिरे और ज़ख्म आए मुझे

मैं घर से तेरी तमन्ना पहन के जब निकलूँ
बरहना[3] शहर में कोई नज़र न आए मुझे

मैं अपने दिल से निकालूँ ख़्याल किस-किसका
जो तू नहीं तो कोई और याद आए मुझे

वो मेहरबाँ[4] है तो इक़रार क्यूँ नहीं करता
वो बदगुमाँ[5] है तो सौ बार आज़माए मुझे।

---

1. चमत्कार, 2. पत्थर, 3. निर्वस्त्र, 4. उदार, 5. भ्रमित

Qateel Shifai

May my love show this miracle too
That I should feel the hurt when the stone hits
you

Whenever I leave home wrapped in the thoughts
of you
I shouldn't find naked in the city anybody else
too

The thoughts of how many can I expel from my
heart
If not yours, it will be somebody else's thought

If he loves me, then why doesn't he accept?
If he is annoyed, let him put me through an acid
test

क़तील शिफ़ाई

उस अदा से भी हूँ मैं आशना, तुझे जिस प' इतना ग़रूर है
मैं जियूँगा तेरे बग़ैर भी, मुझे ज़िन्दगी का शऊर है

न हवस मुझे मै-ए-नाब[1] की, न तलब सवा-औ-सहाब[2] की
तिरे चश्म-ए-नाज़ की खैर हो, मुझे बे पिये ही सरूर है

जो समझ लिया तुझे बावफा तो फिर इसमें तेरी भी क्या ख़ता
ये ख़लल है मेरे दिमाग़ का, ये मिरी नज़र का क़सूर है

कोई बात वो दिल में ठान के, न उलझ पड़े तिरी शान से
वो नियाज़मंद[3] जो सर-ब-ख़म[4] कई दिन से तेरे हुज़ूर हैं।

---

1. ख़ालिस शराब, 2. समीर और वन, 3. आज्ञाकारी, 4. नतमस्तक।

Qateel Shifai

The art of which you are so proud, I know that
art too
I know how to live, and I will live without you

I need neither the pure wine, nor do I hanker after
the breezes of spring
Long live your beauteous eye, I remain drunk
without drinking

You are not to blame for it, it was I who took
you for a person trustworthy
It was a disorder of my mind, a fault of my sight
verily

May I, your faithful one, never do aught
That is unworthy or your thought

Ahmed Faraz

(1931-)

Ahmed Faraz is the greatest living Urdu poet. Coming from a Pathan family, Faraz was born in 1931 in Nowshera (Pakistan). He studied Urdu and Persian at Peshawar University. A genuine and a great modern poet, he says that he writes only when he is compelled from inside. Like Faiz Ahmed Faiz, Faraz has strong political views and he expresses them forcefully. In fact, Faraz, in a very large measure, is a poet in the tradition of Faiz. In his poetry, one finds romanticism, modernism and radicalism all existing side by side. For his political views, he was jailed by the Zia-ul-Haq government, the charge being that he had opposed the military regime, which he had. Once he was arrested immediately after reciting a poem at a mushaira. All this reminds one of Faiz, who served long terms in jail. He was exiled by the Zia regime. Like Faiz again, he wrote some of his best poetry in exile. (Faiz had written his best poetry in jail.)

Faraz stayed for three years in Europe and Canada before returning to Pakistan, where he was appointed chairman of the Pakistan Book Foundation, a position he held for many years. Faraz was honoured with 'Hilal-e-Intiaz' in 2004 for the great contribution he had made to Urdu literature. Faraz was however soon disenchanted with the Musharraf regime's policies and returned this award. He said that his conscience will not forgive him if he remained a mute spectator to what was happening around him. "The least, I can do" says Faraz " is to let the regime know where I stand in the eyes of the people whose fundamental rights have been misused."

Like Faiz in his lifetime, Faraz is a frequent visitor to India, and is held in high esteem. High quality of his poetry and his simple style which common people can understand have made him quite popular. His presence at a mushaira is enough to hold the audience till the end.

His first collection of poems 'Tanha Tanha' appeared in 1958. In all he has published ten collection of poems in addition to a collection of plays and numerous articles. His other collections include 'Janaan Janaan' 'Nabeena Shahr Mein' and 'Dard Ashob'. His works were published by a university in U.A.E. in four volumes.

अहमद फ़राज़

रंज़िश ही सही, दिल ही दुखाने के लिए आ
आ फिर से मुझे छोड़ के जाने के लिए आ

कुछ तो मिरे पिन्दार-ए-मुहब्बत[1] का भरम रख
तू भी तो कभी मुझको मनाने के लिए आ

पहले से मरासिम[2] न सही, फिर भी कभी तो
रस्म-ओ-रह-ए-दुनिया ही निभाने के लिए आ

किस-किस को बताएँगे जुदाई का सबब हम
तू मुझसे ख़फ़ा है, तो ज़माने के लिए आ

इक उम्र से हूँ लज़्ज़त-ए-गिरिया[3] से भी महरूम
ऐ-राहत-ए-जाँ! मुझको रुलाने के लिए आ

अब तक दिल-ए-खुशफहम को तुझसे हैं उमीदें
ये आखिरी शम्मएँ भी बुझाने के लिए आ।

1. प्रेम में स्वाभिमान, 2. सम्बन्ध, 3. रोना

Ahmed Faraz

You may be cross with me, but to hurt me, if nothing else, do come still
Do come to leave me at your will

Let me at least some pride in my love retain
Let you too sometime come to bring me round and my friend remain

Our relations may not be now as cordial as of yore
Still, let you come at least for formality's sake and
Show the world that they are like they were before

It is extremely difficult to explain the cause of our separation to everybody
Come for the sake of the world, if with me you are angry

For a long time now, I have not had the luxury of weeping
Come and make me cry, O my comforter, if else for nothing

I still have illusion, I still have hope from you
Come and blow out this last candle too.

अहमद फ़राज़

अब के हम बिछड़े तो शायद कभी ख़्वाबों में मिलें
जिस तरह सूखे हुए फूल किताबों में मिलें

तू खुदा है, न मिरा इश्क़ फ़रिश्तों जैसा
दोनों इंसाँ हैं तो क्यूँ इतने हिजाबों[1] में मिलें

ग़म-ए-दुनिया भी ग़म-ए-यार में शामिल कर लो
नश्शा बढ़ता है शराबें जो शराबों में मिलें

ढूँढ़ उजड़े हुए लोगों में वफ़ा के मोती
ये खज़ाने तुझे मुमकिन है खराबों[2] में मिलें।

आज हम दार पे खेंचे गए जिन बातों पर
क्या अजब कल वो ज़माने को निसाबों[3] में मिलें

1. पर्दों, 2. खंडहर, 3. पाठ्यक्रम

Ahmed Faraz

Like withered flowers in the books, it seems
If separated now, we might meet only in dreams

Neither is my love like that of an angel, nor do
you partake of divinity
We are both humans, so why meet secretly?

Let the sorrows of the world and sorrows of love
combine
A cocktail is certainly more intoxicating than a
single wine,

Look for the pearls of fidelity only in the people
run aground
Only in the ruins can these treasures be found

Who knows tomorrow they may be found in the
world's syllabi—
The things for which today we are condemned
to die.

अहमद फ़राज़

अब के ऋतु बदली तो खुशबू का सफर देखेगा कौन
ज़ख्म फूलों की तरह महकेंगे, पर देखेगा कौन

देखना सब रक़्स-ए-बिस्मिल[1] में मगन हो जाएँगे
जिस तरफ से तीर आएगा उधर देखेगा कौन

ज़ख्म जितने भी थे सब मंसूब क़ातिल से हुए
तेरे हाथों के निशाँ ऐ चारागर देखेगा कौन।

मेरी आवाज़ों के साए मेरे बाम-ओ-दर[2] प' हैं
मेरे लफ्ज़ों में उतरकर मेरा घर देखेगा कौन

हम चिराग़-ए-शब ही जब ठहरे तो फिर क्या सोचना
रात थी किसका मुकद्दर और सहर देखेगा कौन

आ फ़सील-ए-शहर[3] से देखें ग़नीम-ए-शहर[4] को
शहर जलता हो तो तुझको बाम पर देखेगा कौन

हर कोई अपनी हवा में मस्त फिरता है 'फ़राज़'
शहर-ए-ना-पुरसाँ[5] में तेरी चश्म-ए-तर देखेगा कौन

---

1. घायल का नृत्य, 2. छत और दरवाज़े, 3. शहर की दीवार, 4. शहर का प्रतिद्वंद्वी, 5. जिसे कोई न पूछता हो।

Ahmed Faraz

This time, when the season changes, who will
witness the arrival of spring
And watch the wound-like flowers blooming which
the season will bring

You will see that everybody will watch the wounds
of the injured man like a good game,
And nobody will know from where the arrow came

All the wounds will be ascribed to the murderer,
obviously
Your finger-prints, O messiah, nobody is going to
see,

The echoes of my voice will be heard around my
door-step and ceiling
Nobody will care to enter my words and see the
house itself and know my feeling

If we are merely the candle that burns up at night,
then the matter ends there,
Nobody will know who was fated to be in the
night and who was to see the morning fair

Come, let us from the boundary wall of the city,
city's enemies see
For, when the city is burning, who'll care to see
you on your terrace, O pretty,

Everybody is taking airs, obsessed with himself, here
Who'll in this uncaring city, O Faraz, for your wet
eyes care!

Parveen Shakir
(1952-1995)

सुन्दर कोमल सपनों की बारात गुज़र गई, जनानां
धूप आँखों तक आ पहुँची है रात गुज़र गई, जानानां

(The procession of soft and lovely dreams has passed, my love, and the sun is already high on the sky, my dear)

The moment we read this couplet, we are aware of a new voice in Urdu poetry, a voice that is fresh and pleasing. This is the voice of Parvin Shakir, one of the remarkable poets of the sub-continent. One is struck by the fact that while Pakistan has a number of very good lady poets like Kishwar Naheed, Fehmida Raiz and Parveen Shakir, we in India cannot lay such claim.

Parveen Shakir's case is very tragic. She was killed in a road accident in her prime. She was born in a traditional religious family in Karachi in 1952. Her family believed in simplicity and sharing. Her father was a man of relatively liberal views and she was allowed to move out without pardah (veil). She had her education in Karachi and when in college, she acquainted herself with great works of poetry and prose. She started her literary career as an essayist. It was only when she wrote a poem on a certain occasion in the college that she discovered her true vocation. After that she participated in many poetry competitions and won prizes. She was also writing for the radio. However it was the well-known poet, Ahmed Nadeem Qasmi who was then the editor of 'Fanoon', who gave her a real break. He not only published her ghazals, but also gave her great encouragement. Besides simplicity and freshness, Parveen's poetry has great intensity and clarity of images. She became popular with her very first collection 'Khushboo' which went into three editions in just one month. Her three other collections are 'Sadberg', 'Khudkalami' and Tankar'.

Parveen Shakir was working in a senior position in the customs department of Pakistan when the fatal road accident took place in 1995.

परवीन शाकिर

चेहरा मेरा था निगाहें उसकी
खामुशी में भी वो बातें उसकी

मेरे चेहरे पे ग़ज़ल लिखती गईं
शे'र कहती हुई आँखें उसकी

ऐसे मौसम भी गुज़ारे हमने
सुबहें जब अपनी थीं शामें उसकी

फ़ैसला मौजे-हवा[1] ने लिखा
आँधियाँ मेरी, बहारें उसकी

दूर रह के भी सदा रहती हैं
मुझको थामे हुए बाँहें उसकी

नींद इस सोच से टूटी अक्सर[2]
किस तरह कटती हैं रातें उसकी

---

1. हवा की लहरें, 2. प्रायः।

Parvin Shakir

The face was mine, his the eyes
Even in silence, talking to him, would, I surmise

It all got written on my face automatically
His eyes went on writing poetry

Such seasons too have I seen
When mornings were mine, but the evenings his
have been

The blowing breeze gifted us two different things
The high winds to me, to him the springs

Even when from him I am away
In his arms, safe I stay

Often, I am startled in my sleep
Thinking, how doth he during the nights keep

परवीन शाकिर

अब कैसी परदादारी ख़बर आम हो चुकी
माँ की रिदा[1] तो दिन हुए नीलाम हो चुकी

सूरज भी उसको ढूंढ़ के वापस चला गया
अब हम भी घर को लौट चलें शाम हो चुकी

आँखें हैं और सुबह तलक तेरा इंतज़ार
मश्अल-ब-दस्त[2] रात तेरे नाम हो चुकी

शमले[3] संभालते ही रहे मसलहत-पसंद[4]
होना था जिसको प्यार में बदनाम हो चुकी।

---

1. चादर, 2. मशाल उठाए हुए, 3. पगड़ी, 4. भला-बुरा समझाने वाले।

Parvin Shakir

Why hide it, the people already know
That our mother's covering-cloth was sold away, long ago

The sun too has gone back, failing to find him anywhere
Let us also get back home, for the evening is already here

The eyes have waited for you till the dawn
Holding the candle in hand, the entire night is gone

The discreet one is busy keeping his turban tidy
She is in love, and she is disgraced already

बारिश हुई तो फूलों के तन चाक[1] हो गए
मौसम के हाथ भीग के सफ़्फ़ाक[2] हो गए

बादल को क्या ख़बर है कि बारिश की चाह में
कितने बुलंद-ओ-बाला शजर[3] ख़ाक हो गए

जुगनू को दिन के वक़्त परखने की ज़िद करें
बच्चे हमारे अहद[4] के चालाक हो गए

लहरा रही है बर्फ़ की चादर हटा के घास
सूरज की शह पे तिनके भी बेबाक़ हो गए

जब भी ग़रीबे-शहर से कुछ गुफ्तगू हुई
लहजे हवाए-शाम के नमनाक हो गए

बस्ती में जितने आब-गज़ीदा[5] थे सब-के-सब
दरिया के रुख बदलते ही तैराक हो गए।

---

1. फटना, 2. निष्ठुर, 3. ऊँचें-नीचे पेड़, 4. काल, 5. पानी से भयभीत।

Parvin Shakir

As it rained, the flowers had holes in their bodies made
Drenched by the weather, they made a tougher grade

How would the cloud know that waiting for rain
So many tall and mighty trees have been on the ground lain

They insist on testing the firefly in daylight
Present-day children have readily become bright

The grass is dancing after the snow-cover is gone
Even the straws have become bold, being by the sun egged on

Whenever a conversation with those, away from home, it had
The evening breeze became moist and sad

All those who would out of fear, the waters shun
Have become swimmers after the river has changed direction

Shaharyar

(1936-)

Shaharyar, whose full name is Akhlaq Mohammad Khan Shaharyar is held in high esteem among the present day Urdu poets. He is a very significant poet writing in the tradition of modern poetry. Unlike his many contemporaries, he is not aligned with any particular social ideology. Even his modernism is not strictly wedded to modernist school. He does not equate modernism with denial of social responsibility. Moreover, he has no hesitation in employing classical style and language.

Shaharyar in his poetry, seeks self realization. Also, he tries to understand the predicament of the modern man and the problems he faces. He expresses the psychological conflicts of modern man and his spiritual sufferings. The strength of his poetry lies in vividly expressing contemporary problems. This, he is able to do because of the intensity and freshness of his thought and tone. He is not concerned with conclusion, nor does he give a message.

Shaharyar was born in a village in Bareilly. After his early education in Bulandsahar and Aligarh, he worked for some time as a literary assistant in Anjuman-e-Taraqqi Urdu. He joined Aligarh University as a lecturer in Urdu and became a professor there in 1980. His first collection appeared in 1965. Shaharyar's other poetic works are "Satvan Dar" (1969), "Hijar ke Mausam" (1978) and "Khawab ka Dar Band Hai" which won him Sahitya-Academy award in 1987. Shaharyar has distinctly individual style and recites poetry in a low tone. He is generally taciturn and avoids loudness in poetry. He is an intellectual. Shaharyar has written some memorable ghazals for the films too.

शहरयार

तुम्हारे शहर में कुछ भी हुआ नहीं है क्या
कि तुमने चीख़ों को सचमुच सुना नहीं है क्या

तमाम ख़ल्के खुदा इस जगह रुकी क्यूँ हैं
यहाँ से आगे कोई रास्ता नहीं है क्या

लहूलुहान सभी कर रहे हैं सूरज को
किसी को खौफ़ यहाँ रात का नहीं है क्या

मैं इक ज़माने से हैरान हूँ कि हाकिम-ए-शहर
जो हो रहा है उसे देखता नहीं है क्या

उजाड़ते हैं जो नादाँ इसे उजड़ने दो
कि उजड़ा शहर दोबारा बसा नहीं है क्या।

Shaharyar

Has nothing whatever happened in your city?
Have you not heard the shrieks, really?

Why is everybody stranded here
Is there no way out whatever!

Everybody is giving a bloody face to the sun
Why, is nobody afraid of the night here, none?

For sometime, I am angered that the commander of the city
Just doesn't know what is happening really.

They who lay the city waste, let them do their worst
Does a ruined town never again into life burst!

शहरयार

तेरे सिवा भी मुझे कोई याद आने वाला था
मैं वरना यूँ हिज्र से कब घबराने वाला था

जानबूझकर सोच-समझ कर मैंने भुला दिया
हर वो किस्सा जो दिल को बहलाने वाला था

मुझको नदामत[1] बस इस पर है कि लोग बहुत खुश हैं
उस लमहे को खोकर जो पछताने वाला था

ये तो खैर हुई दरिया ने रुख तब्दील किया
मेरा शहर भी उसकी ज़द में आने वाला था

इक-इक करके सब रस्ते कितने सुनसान हुए
याद आया मैं लंबे सफ़र पे जाने वाला था।

---

1. शर्मसारी

Shaharyar

Apart from you, I had somebody else too in my
mind
Otherwise this separation I would not so
intolerable find

Each such incident I deliberately forgot
That could possibly comfort my heart

I am ashamed of the fact that people are happy
After losing the moment for which they should
have been sorry

Luckily, the river changed its course
Otherwise my town too was going to feel its force

One by one, all the roads were deserted
And I was going to set out on a long journey,
I remembered.

Bashir Badra

(1935-)

उजाले अपनी यादों के हमारे साथ रहने दो
न जाने किस गली में ज़िंदगी की शाम हो जाए

(Let the light of your memories stay with us
Who knows in which alley the nightfall of life may overtake us)

Coming to limelight with this couplet, Bashir Badra is now a regular feature at every important mushaira in the country and even abroad. He was born in 1935 and had his higher education at Aligarh University from where he took a Ph.D. Degree on Urdu ghazal after Independence. He had started publishing in 'Savera' (Lahore) and 'Naya Adab' (Karachi). Bashir Badra was a disciple of Gian Chand Girdab whom he holds in high esteem. Though he often writes on modern themes like alienation of man and the loss of his identity in the present-day world, he is essentially a poet of love and beauty. Some of the stock images of romantic poetry like the moon, the star and the flowers repeatedly occur in his poetry. He is a poet of the ghazal, and he is one of those who reestablished ghazal in Urdu poetry when its place of primacy was threatened by the ascendancy of the nazm. He taught at Meerut where his house was burnt down in a communal riot.

Bashir Badra has unique tarannum (way of singing his ghazals), which makes him popular at mushairas. He is good at pictorial presentation as well. He makes some incisive observations on the life of man in our industrial age. Also, there is a throw-back to the life in the past in a small town. The popularity of his poetry at one time made him think that he was at par with Meer and Ghalib. This attracted a very hostile notice from the critics. Unfortunately, his writing in recent years has lacked the quality of his earlier poetry of great sensuousness and lyrical excellence. 'Ikai' (1969), 'Image" (1973) and 'Aamad' (1985) are his well-known poetic collections.

बशीर बद्र

कोई फूल धूप की पत्तियों में हरे रिबन से बँधा हुआ
वो ग़ज़ल का लहजा नया नया, न कहा हुआ न सुना हुआ

जिसे ले गई है अभी हवा, वो वरक़ था दिल की किताब का
कहीं आँसुओं से मिटा हुआ, कहीं आँसुओं से लिखा हुआ

कई मील रेत को काटकर कोई मौज फूल खिला गई
कोई पेड़ प्यास से मर रहा है नदी के पास खड़ा हुआ

मिरे साथ जुगनू है हमसफ़र, मगर उस शरर[1] की बिसात क्या
यह चिराग़ कोई चिराग़ है न जला हुआ न बुझा हुआ।

1. चिंगारी

Bashir Badra

Like a flower wrapped in sunlight and tied with
a green ribbon
It is a ghazal in a new vein, neither heard before,
nor written

The page, just blown away, was a page from the
book of the heart
In part written with tears, by tears blotted out
in part

Cutting through miles of sand somewhere a wave
has brought the flower to bloom
While to die of thirst on the river bank itself is
some tree's doom

On this journey, I am accompanied by a firefly,
but what use is a flicker after all
It is a candle, which is neither lit-up nor blown
out can we call.

बशीर बद्र

यूँ ही बेसबब न फिरा करो, कोई शाम घर भी रहा करो
वो ग़ज़ल की अच्छी किताब है उसे चुपके-चुपके पढ़ा करो

कोई हाथ भी न मिलाएगा जो गले मिलोगे तपाक से
ये नए मिज़ाज का शहर है ज़रा फ़ासले से मिला करो

कभी हुस्न पर्दानशीं भी हो ज़रा आशिक़ाना लिबास में
जो मैं बन सँवर के कहीं चलूँ, मिरे साथ तुम भी चला करो

नहीं बेहिजाब[1] वो चाँद-सा कि नज़र का कोई असर न हो
उसे इतनी गर्मि-ए-शौक़[2] से बड़ी देर तक न तका करो।

---

1. बेपरदा, 2. उत्सुकता, लगन।

Bashir Badra

Don't be wandering around aimlessly, stay some
evening at home too,
That is a good book of ghazals, read it silently
wrapped unto you

Nobody will even shake hand with you, if you
try to embrace warmly
This is town with a new culture, meet people here
from a distance only

Let your beauty too be dressed up sometime, in
a lover's attire
Let you also accompany me, when all made up,
I go somewhere

She, when unveiled, unlike the moon, is not
unaffected by being seen
Don't be looking at her for such a long time with
eyes so keen.

Nida Fazli

(1938)

दुनिया जिसे कहते हैं जादू का खिलौना है
मिल जाए तो मिट्टी है खो जाए तो सोना है

(This world is a magical toy, so to say
Gold when you lose it, when possessed it's dust and clay)

The writer of this wonderful couplet, which is perhaps his best, was born in Gwalior in 1938. He had his education and took a masters degree from there. His father who too was a poet, migrated to Pakistan, but Nida choose to stay back in India. He felt fascinated by bhajans of Mira, Surdas and the poetry of Kabir, and found in their writing something very different from the run-of-the mill Urdu poetry. He was quite dissatisfied with the Daagh school of writing, which he found wanting in the context of present-day problems.

Nida Fazli is a well-known lyricist, writing for films. His ghazals and nazms have been sung by most of the ghazal singers of the country and Jagjit Singh seems to be particularly impressed with him. He has written some doha's also. Nida Fazli uses, simple, colloquial language free from Persianised diction and compound words. He wrote some critical essays on his contemporaries, which annoyed poets like Sahir, Sardar Jafri and Kaifi Azmi.

It was Kamal Amrohi who gave him a chance to write for films. Writing songs for films gave him much needed money but he soon found the job mechanical and concentrated more on serious poetry. He negates partition, is against communalism and fundamentalism. One finds nostalgic childhood imagery, as also search for meaning, contradictions of present-day life and scatthing comments on our urban existence recurring in his poetry. He has written twenty four books. Apart from poetry, he has also written a novel, 'Deevaron ke Beech'. His book of criticism is titled 'Mulakaten'.

निदा फ़ाज़ली

दुनिया जिसे कहते हैं, जादू का खिलौना है
मिल जाए तो मिट्टी है, खो जाए तो सोना है

आवारा मिज़ाजी ने फैला दिया आँगन को
आकाश की चादर है, धरती का बिछौना है

अच्छा-सा कोई मौसम, तन्हा सा कोई आलम
हर वक़्त का रोना तो, बेकार का रोना है।

बरसात का बादल तो, दीवाना है क्या जाने
किस राह से बचना है, किस छत को भिगोना है

Nida Fazli

This world is a magical toy, so to say
Gold, when you lose it, when possessed, it is dust
and clay

My vagabonding has spread me far and wide
The sky in my canopy, and the earth to me doth
my bedding provide

Looking for moments of solitude, looking for season
at its prime!—
It is no use crying and cribbing all the time.

Which road to avoid and where to rain—
The cloud of the rainy season knows not, it is
insane.

निदा फ़ाज़ली

ख़ुदा ख़ामोश है

बहुत-से काम हैं—
लिपटी हुई धरती को फैलावें
दरख़्तों को उगाएँ, डालियों पर फूलमहकावें
पहाड़ों को करीने से लगाएँ
चाँद लटकाएँ
ख़्लाओं के सिरे पर नीलगू आकाश फैलाएँ
सितारों को करे रोशन
हवाओं को गति देवें
चमकते पत्थरों को पंख देकर नग़मग़ी देवें
लबों को मुस्कुराहट, अंखड़ियों को रोशनी देवें
सड़क पर डोलती छायाओं को ज़िंदगी देवें
खुदा खामोश है
तुम आओ तो तख़लीक हो दुनिया
मैं इतने सारे कामों को अकेला कर नहीं सकता।

Nida Fazli

God is Silent

There are so many things to do—
We have to give width to this shrivelled up earth,
Trees have to be planted and their branches laden
with fruits,
The hills have to be given some order
And the sky is to be given a moon,
And we have to cover the empty spaces with blue
sky,
Let us give speed to the winds,
And feather and flight to the shining stones;
We have to put smile on the lips and light in the
people's eyes.
And put life in the shadows walking on the road—
God is inert
Only if you join in, can we create a new world,
Alone, I cannot do it all.

निदा फ़ाज़ली

ऐलान

मस्जिदों-मन्दिरों की दुनिया में
मुझको पहचानते कहाँ हैं लोग
रोज़ मैं चाँद बनके आता हूँ
दिन में सूरज-सा जगमगाता हूँ
खनखनाता हूँ माँ के गहनों में
हँसता रहता हूँ छिपके बहनों में
मैं ही मज़दूर के पसीने में
मैं ही बरसात के महीने में
मेरी तकरीर आँख का आँसू
मेरी तहरीर जिस्म का जादू
मस्जिदों-मन्दिरों की दुनिया में
मुझको पहचानते नहीं जब लोग
मैं ज़मीनों को बेज़िया करके
आसमानों में लौट जाता हूँ
मैं खुदा बनके कहर ढाता हूँ।

Nida Fazli

A Declaration

In the world of the temples and the mosques
People know me not;
I come here in the shape of the moon every night
And during the day, in the form of the sun
I shine in the ornaments of the mothers
And smile gently through the sisters,
I am present in the sweat of the workers
And also present in the rainy season,
My speech brings tears to the eye
My writings cast a spell on men and women.
But in the world of the temples and the mosques
When people know me not,
I plunge this world into darkness
And to the skies return—
In the form of God then, this world I burn.

निदा फ़ाज़ली

कराची एक माँ है

कराची एक माँ है
बम्बई बिछुड़ा हुआ बेटा
ये रिश्ता प्यार का पाकीज़ा रिश्ता है जिसे अब तक
न कोई तोड़ पाया है
न कोई तोड़ पाएगा
न मेरी माँ कभी तलवार ताने रन में आई है
न मैंने अपनी माँ के सामने बन्दूक उठाई है
ये कैसा शोर-ओ-हंगामा है ये किसकी लड़ाई है
कराची एक माँ है।

Nida Fazli

Karachi is home to a mother

Karachi is home to a mother
And Mumbai to a son, separated from her,
This relation is a pious relation of affection
Which till date nobody has been able to break
And will never be broken.
Neither has my mother ever come for battle,
Holding sword in hand,
Nor have I ever trained a gun against her
Then, who is fighting whom
And what for is the stir?
Karachi is a mother—...

❐ ❐ ❐